PRAISE FOR
A New Era of Philanthropy

"Through artful storytelling and concrete ideas, *A New Era of Philanthropy* gives the sector a hopeful path forward that … creates truly transformative change. A must-read for anyone in philanthropy, particularly those who question whether and how philanthropic resources can address the current, complex challenges our world faces."

> —NICK TEDESCO, president and chief executive officer of the National Center for Family Philanthropy

"Through expert storytelling and practical suggestions, Abichandani offers a powerful narrative that allows us to reimagine what philanthropy can be—and provides a path to get there."

> —DAN HEATH, *New York Times* best-selling author of *Made to Stick* and *Switch*

"Nourishing, stimulating, and incisively sharp, *A New Era of Philanthropy* embodies the creativity and connection that must guide philanthropy moving forward. Do yourself a favor and read this book."

> —PIA INFANTE, co-executive director of the Trust-Based Philanthropy Project

"Dimple Abichandani challenges us to imagine how foundations and donors can break from conventional practices and instead catalyze deeper, transformative change to foster a thriving multiracial democracy, repair past harms, and create a sustainable future.… [S]he proposes a new blueprint for philanthropy that meets the moment."

> —DON CHEN, president of the Surdna Foundation

"A beautiful, bold, and compelling invitation to reimagine philanthropy as we know it."

> —SARITA GUPTA, vice president of US Programs at the Ford Foundation

"*A New Era of Philanthropy* offers essential practices to help us consider who we must be and what we must do if we are serious about building a world of more justice, fairness, and abundance."

—LEAH HUNT-HENDRIX, cofounder of the Solidaire Network and Way to Win and coauthor of *Solidarity*

"Dimple's invitation is to engage, and—through practice—to transform philanthropy, and to be transformed in the process. As I read this book full of generous wisdom, storytelling, and guidance, I could palpably feel this New Era arriving."

—RAJASVINI BHANSALI, executive director of the Solidaire Network

"*A New Era of Philanthropy* calls philanthropy to account with hard-won wisdom, deep care, and inspiring curiosity.... We must answer this urgent call to leave the gilded era behind, and build a new, collective future together."

—BAILEY MALONE, executive director of the CS Fund

"A treasure trove.... Must-read wisdom for every donor and funder, from a voice we can trust."

—VANESSA PRIYA DANIEL, founder of the Groundswell Fund and author of *Unrig the Game*

"Dimple is the doula our sector has been waiting for, transitioning philanthropy from an outdated model to the potential and possibilities that meet the challenges of our world today."

—PHUONG QUACH, principal at NPAG

"… a foundational text for everyone in philanthropy today. Dimple's stories, frameworks, and exercises make sense of today while guiding us in the work we need to do for a future that is more just and equitable."

—SAYU BHOJWANI, board chair of the North Star Fund, founder of Women's Democracy Lab, and author of *People Like Us*

"*A New Era of Philanthropy* turns a sharp eye on the foundational myths and assumptions that shape how the philanthropic sector operates and invites us to imagine what we could achieve if resource stewards adopted a proposed set of principles and practices that reflect and enable our highest aspirations."

—MANDY VAN DEVEN, narrative and philanthropy expert

"… a roadmap to show how philanthropy can meet the current moment. … Donors, program officers, and trustees as well as nonprofit and movement leaders will benefit from this book."

—DEEPA IYER, author of *Social Change Now*

"This book has the potential to transform everything we thought we knew about 'philanthropy as usual.'"

—REGAN PRITZKER, board co-president of the Libra Foundation and board member of the Kataly Foundation

"Abichandani offers a compelling and actionable pathway for reimagining conventional approaches to philanthropy.… She lovingly reminds us that, no matter your starting point, there are many ways to take a step forward to prepare ourselves— and our sector—for a new era."

—SHAADY SALEHI, co-executive director of the Trust-Based Philanthropy Project

"Abichandani invites us to engage with the central question of how we transform the complicated legacy of extractive wealth into one grounded in justice and sustainability.… a compelling centerpiece of any course for the next generation of nonprofit and philanthropic leaders."

—MOLLY SCHULTZ HAFID, adjunct associate professor at the NYU Wagner Graduate School of Public Service and executive director of the Butler Family Fund

"Dimple Abichandani provides readers the historical context that unduly constrains the practice of giving today. In doing so, she invites us to chart a new and more generous path forward. This new way is rooted in solidarity, care, and trust."

—CARMEN ROJAS, president and CEO of the Marguerite Casey Foundation

"If you're wondering what 'the deal' is with philanthropy, there isn't a better place to start."

—FARHAD EBRAHIMI, founder and president of the Chorus Foundation

"Dimple Abichandani has given us many gifts in *A New Era of Philanthropy*, inviting us to move beyond the critique of philanthropy and into action, with practices that allow us to live into the future we want to bring about."

—CASSIE ROBINSON, director at Arising Quo and associate director of Emerging Futures at the Joseph Rowntree Foundation

"*A New Era of Philanthropy* is a gift for those committed to truth telling and using philanthropy as a tool to repair and build a more equitable society."

—EDGAR VILLANUEVA, author of *Decolonizing Wealth* and founder/CEO of the Decolonizing Wealth Project and Liberated Capital

"A stellar practitioner of innovative ways of giving, Abichandani instructs and supports readers who envision philanthropy doing the 'most good' rather than just 'some good.' . . . Put down that Gospel of Wealth and move into real philanthropy that is driven by the common good instead of an egocentric tax scam."

—RINKU SEN, executive director of the Narrative Initiative

"With keen observations and insights, [this book] point[s] the way to what a modernized philanthropy can be."

—DENNIS QUIRIN, executive director of the Raikes Foundation

". . . a must-read. Dimple describes how philanthropists cling to old assumptions and practices that curtail effectiveness.... [S]he offers interactive prompts we can use to excise what's not working and begin to rebuild philanthropy from the ground up."

—CRYSTAL HAYLING, *Inside Philanthropy's* 2021 Foundation Leader of the Year and one of *Inside Philanthropy's* 2023 50 Most Powerful Women in Philanthropy

". . . one of the most important reads of the year."

—MARCUS F. WALTON, president and CEO of Grantmakers for Effective Organizations

"Philanthropy can help bring forth the multiracial democracy we all desire and deserve: Abichandani's work can help us get there."

—DEEPAK BHARGAVA, president of the JPB Foundation

A NEW ERA OF PHILANTHROPY

A NEW ERA OF PHILANTHROPY

Ten Practices to Transform
Wealth into a More Just
and Sustainable Future

DIMPLE ABICHANDANI

North Atlantic Books

Huichin, unceded Ohlone land
Berkeley, California

North Atlantic Books
Huichin, unceded Ohlone land
2526 Martin Luther King Jr Way
Berkeley, CA 94704 USA
www.northatlanticbooks.com

Cover art © mycola via Getty Images
Cover art by Jason Arias/Jasmine Hromjak
Book design by Happenstance Type-O-Rama

Printed in the United States of America

A New Era of Philanthropy: Ten Practices to Transform Wealth into a More Just and Sustainable Future is sponsored and published by North Atlantic Books, an educational nonprofit based in the unceded Ohlone land Huichin (Berkeley, CA) that collaborates with partners to develop cross-cultural perspectives; nurture holistic views of art, science, the humanities, and healing; and seed personal and global transformation by publishing work on the relationship of body, spirit, and nature.

North Atlantic Books's publications are distributed to the US trade and internationally by Penguin Random House Publisher Services. For further information, visit our website at www.northatlanticbooks.com.

Library of Congress Cataloging-in-Publication Data
Names: Abichandani, Dimple author
Title: A new era of philanthropy : ten practices to transform wealth into a
    more just and sustainable future / Dimple Abichandani.
Description: Berkeley, CA : North Atlantic Books, [2025] | Includes
    bibliographical references and index. | Summary: "A guide to equitable
    philanthropy for funders, foundations, and nonprofit leaders"-- Provided
    by publisher.
Identifiers: LCCN 2024042700 (print) | LCCN 2024042701 (ebook) | ISBN
    9798889841388 trade paperback | ISBN 9798889841395 ebook
Subjects: LCSH: Charity organization | Charities | Fund raising
Classification: LCC HV40 .A25 2025 (print) | LCC HV40 (ebook) | DDC
    361.706--dc23/eng/20250110
LC record available at https://lccn.loc.gov/2024042700
LC ebook record available at https://lccn.loc.gov/2024042701

The authorized representative in the EU for product safety and compliance is Eucomply OÜ, Pärnu mnt 139b-14, 11317 Tallinn, Estonia, hello@eucompliancepartner.com, +33757690241.

1 2 3 4 5 6 7 8 9 KPC 30 29 28 27 26 25

For Mom, Anand, and Sumi—
for all the abundance you bring to my life.

CONTENTS

In this truth, in this faith we trust.
For while we have our eyes on the future,
History has its eyes on us.

This is the era of just redemption.
We feared at its inception.
We did not feel prepared to be the heirs
Of such a terrifying hour.
But within it we found the power
To author a new chapter,
To offer hope and laughter to ourselves.

—excerpt from inaugural poet Amanda Gorman,
"The Hill We Climb"

INTRODUCTION

This book is a full-hearted invitation in times of crisis and opportunity to accelerate the emergence of a new era of philanthropy. A philanthrophy that sees its purpose as transformation: transforming wealth into more just and sustainable futures; transforming unjust systems into systems devoted to flourishing; transforming how we see and do the work of philanthropy, from disparate and isolated efforts to collective and interdependent progress.

Near my house in Alameda, California, is an old naval base, decommissioned decades ago. At least once a week I walk by the water. The base, a striking landscape of old wars, with runways and abandoned warehouses, is in a state of reimagination, a place in between the past and the future. A new chapter is emerging, shaped by community voice: affordable housing, a food bank, and an art center. At the end of the former runway, where warplanes once took off, an ecological park named De-Pave will return the land to its original habitat, with marshlands standing ready to absorb rising sea levels.

This landscape reminds me of how we rarely build the future from scratch. Rather, we repurpose the old infrastructures, infusing them with our contemporary values, visions, and dreams. Sometimes the "new" is a necessary return.

Like my home island, philanthropy—the sector of individual donors and institutional foundations allocating private resources toward the public good—is also in transition. While it may not be visible on the surface, over the last decade of crises, we've collectively been evolving and forging a new era of philanthropy. Wherever your starting point is, chances are you picked up this book because you too are wondering if philanthropy can be transformed—and transformative. Whether you work in institutional philanthropy or finance, are one of the majority of Americans who donate to nonprofits, or are a steward of some of the $124 trillion that will transfer between generations by 2048, you want to give in ways that can meet this moment and contribute to a more just future.[1] You want to leave behind a world in which today's children, and their children and their children's children, not only have a shot at survival, but will thrive. With a connection to both resources and social change, you grasp the unique stakes in our times, and understand the role that financial resources can play in making progress. If you are exploring how you, personally, and philanthropy, collectively, can deploy these resources toward change, this book is for you.

The Old Era

To understand where philanthropy is going, we must first understand how it is we came to be here. This story has many beginnings, but when I consider who has shaped modern philanthropy the most, I think about Andrew Carnegie.

On a recent trip to Pacific Grove, California, I brought my laptop to the local library to work on this book and was struck to look up and see a framed portrait of Andrew Carnegie (1835–1919), the "father of modern philanthropy," looking at me, in the last remaining Carnegie library in Monterey County. I kept wondering why this portrait was hanging in this public library in a small seaside California town in 2024.

The simplest answer is that today we remember Carnegie because he wanted to be remembered, as a patron and a saint, the "patron saint" of libraries. Carnegie funded the building of 2,509 libraries in English-speaking countries, including 1,679 in the United States.[2] In 1935, the Carnegie Corporation mailed portraits of Andrew Carnegie to each of the libraries he funded in commemoration of the centennial of his birth.[3]

When people think of philanthropy, they might think of the libraries, or hospital wings, art museums, universities, those announcements on public radio—the list goes on. Philanthropy, private investment for the common good, is a ubiquitous and growing feature of our civic life. It often sounds like an objectively good thing—like building thousands of libraries. Philanthropy is often told as a story of the grand generosity of a wealthy person, and by extension, the benefits to the many of an economic system that by design works for the few. But beneath the surface, there is complexity that we must grapple with: generosity mixed with control, common good with outsized benefits to the wealthiest, and a covering up of the harms that stem from unjust systems.

So, let's scratch the surface. Who was Andrew Carnegie? One of the richest men to ever live, Carnegie was an industrialist credited with building the American steel industry, and a founder of modern philanthropy. He made his unprecedented fortune in part by paying low wages to the workers at his steel plants and crushing the unions that stood up for these workers.[4] The most infamous of these labor disputes took place at Carnegie's Homestead Steel Plant in 1892 after Carnegie approved slashing wages and hiring private police to crush the union.[5] Ten people were killed and many more injured in what was one of the deadliest labor conflicts in the country's history.[6] Carnegie prevailed, wages fell, and workers' hours increased from eight to twelve hours a day, leaving them little time to enjoy the libraries. Union membership at steel mills plummeted as Carnegie's profits soared.[7]

In Carnegie's lifetime, the Homestead Steel strikes stained his reputation. Today, though, he is most often remembered as a generous philanthropist. As we forge a new era of philanthropy for our times, what do we need to know about Andrew Carnegie and his imprint on how social change is resourced today?

Carnegie believed that the wealthy know best, writing that the man of wealth, "is best calculated to produce the most beneficial results for the community . . . bringing to their service his superior wisdom, experience, and ability to administer, doing for them better than they would or could do for themselves."[8] Carnegie's philanthropy wasn't about communities, what they needed, their voices, and their self-determination. This was a philanthropy rooted in the personal experience of the most wealthy and powerful man of his times. He built libraries because *he* benefited from access to a library, the same reason that many of today's donors invest in issues and causes that speak to them personally.

Carnegie's philanthropy was characterized by control: He dictated every aspect of the libraries, including requiring ongoing local funding for the library, approving site locations, even dictating architectural design.[9] By 1908, Carnegie's secretary, James Bertram, had written an entire book to reflect his design preferences, "consistent with good taste": room measurements, lampposts to symbolize enlightenment, and staircases to symbolize the elevation of a person when they read. The mandatory staircases made libraries inaccessible to visitors with disabilities, but communities that did not comply with Carnegie's preferences did not receive funding for their libraries. Carnegie's philanthropy lacked any form of governance or oversight, so these consequential decisions that would impact communities for more than a century to come were his and his alone.

Like so many of us, I have always loved public libraries. My point is not that the libraries Carnegie funded are not a resource, but that we should consider what we lose when our precious civic infrastructure is built without community voice and vision. And we should keep a keen eye on who reaps the benefits from philanthropy.

Philanthropy is inextricable from power, and its introduction into any system is never neutral: It either affirms and amplifies the existing power structures, or challenges and shifts them. Carnegie's philanthropy may have left behind many beautiful libraries, but it also kept unjust systems intact and amplified inequalities. In the segregated South, where African Americans were denied access to libraries and other public institutions, Carnegie funded separate, more modest libraries. Scholar and activist W. E. B. DuBois spoke out against the construction of the Atlanta Carnegie Library, which served white patrons only, noting the injustice of a public facility that refused service to a full third of Atlanta's population.[10]

In Carnegie's time, his philanthropy was understood by many as a tool to cover his exploits, and a way to influence his future legacy. The cover image of *Harper's Weekly* magazine from March 1901 depicts a monstrously large Carnegie stacking his libraries to create a wall that shields the view behind it of smoke and fire rising from his steel plants. The headline reads, "Building a Very Solid Temple of Fame."[11] The *St. Louis Post-Dispatch* editorialized that "Ten thousand 'Carnegie Public Libraries' would not compensate the country for the direct and indirect evils resulting from the Homestead lockout."[12]

Gilded Is Not Gold

Carnegie lived in a time we now know as the Gilded Age. To gild is to "cover thinly with gold leaf or gold paint."[13] Mark Twain coined the term *Gilded Age* to "describe the era's patina of splendor" as well as "the shaky foundations undergirding industrialists' vast accumulation of wealth."[14] "Gilded, after all, is not gold," historian Kimberly Hamlin explains.[15]

The era of philanthropy that Carnegie ushered in is a "gilded philanthropy." It covers unjust systems, purporting to do good, but rarely disturbing who holds power and wealth in our society. It's a philanthropy that says we can have some nice things, like libraries, parks, and concert halls, when and how those who hold extreme wealth want. Gilded philanthropy became a blueprint in Carnegie's time and still informs ours. Some might see it as a failed philanthropy, but in fact it has been successful in its core purpose of mitigating and covering the harms of extreme capitalism.

Gilded philanthropy has stifled our imagination for too long, crowding out all the other more democratic and equitable ways that we can resource the common good. This philanthropy has been wholly about a wealthy individual, most often a white man, setting an agenda for the public good with virtually no governance, accountability, or community input to guide this work. It is a philanthropy that covers this difficult truth: When unjust systems are kept in place, it is the wealthiest and most powerful that benefit.

I think about the interconnected and existential challenges we face today: rising authoritarianism, an accelerating climate crisis, and deepening inequality. While there are ample needs for abundant resources to tackle all of these challenges, gilded philanthropy was not designed to meet the challenges of this moment. The patina has chipped away, revealing cracks in the foundation.

Questions for Our Times

"Do you believe that philanthropy can meet the challenges of our times?"

A few years ago, I started asking this question, inviting rooms of funders to close their eyes and raise their hands if they thought that philanthropy could meet this moment. I can report, from this unscientific experiment, that few people raised their hands. Those that did only lifted their hands halfway and then moved them side to side to indicate a maybe.

These maybes were an exception to this rule I stumbled on. So many of us resourcing social change harbor deep questions: about whether we are doing enough, whether the tool of philanthropy can be liberatory, and about whether we are part of the solution or just another expression of the problem.

I began asking this question of whether philanthropy as it exists today can meet this moment because *I* was personally grappling with it. After two decades of working in some of the most innovative philanthropic organizations, moving resources to brilliant changemakers who are building a more just and sustainable future, my own answer to this question was no. Not today's gilded philanthropy.

Asking this question of my peers helped me realize that I wasn't alone. There is a growing sense that not only is philanthropy not making the difference we seek, but all too often it is part of the problem. I was thinking about this when on a panel in 2023, my co-panelist Maurice Mitchell of the Working Families Party implored funders to step into the urgency of this moment. He reminded us that the house is on fire and that philanthropy needs to "grab a bucket." Agreeing with Maurice's assessment that our collective house is on fire, I couldn't help but wonder, *What does it mean to grab a bucket when you don't believe you can put out the fire?*

———

A few words on the "fire" of our times so that we can better understand the "bucket" that is needed. This book was written in a moment of urgent and intersecting crises: attacks on our democracy, rising inequalities, a climate in crisis, a backdrop of wars, and escalating authoritarianism, extremism, and hate.

Domestically, in the United States we are living out the consequences of an extractive hypercapitalist economy that puts profits before people, of worldviews that see us all as separate, of generations of domination and extraction. We see all around us the harms wrought by systems of greed and exploitation, systems that have not adequately valued life and our planet.

This economy of extreme inequality has fueled a growing philanthropic sector. In the United States alone, philanthropy holds $1.6 trillion in assets, and growing, for the public good.[16] We are in the early years of the Great Wealth Transfer, with Baby Boomers passing on an estimated $124 trillion in wealth to Millennial and Gen Z descendants, and with $18 trillion estimated to go to charitable giving by 2048.[17] How will these tipping-point crises and ever-increasing dollars meet?

To be clear, most of the assets in the philanthropic sector are not moving us toward a more just and sustainable future. In fact, some of these assets are actively deployed to thwart, rather than advance, justice. This book is not aimed at donors who are satisfied with the status quo, or those who long to take us back to some "great" time in the past. It's for the rest of us: the large part of philanthropy—institutions and donors—who grasp the unique urgency of our times and sense that we must make fundamental changes in our sector to build a different future. It is a call to realize the full potential of the resources we have available, including the capital locked away in investments, donor-advised funds, and endowments.

Today as funders consider how to meet the moment, many of us are grappling with questions about wealth, how it is organized, and why so much of it is held in philanthropy. These inquiries help us make sense of old world orders so that we can imagine, dream, and craft new ones. As we deepen our understanding of how we came to be here, we can imagine and plan more ambitiously for how we might redistribute resources to repair and heal a broken world.

Philanthropy's Mandate in a New Era

This book seeks answers to these generative questions: What *is* a philanthropy that meets this urgent moment? And what philanthropic practices go beyond covering up unjust systems to making real, lasting social change?

Philanthropy's mandate is unique. In contrast to other sectors with large amounts of wealth, philanthropy's purpose is not to maintain or grow resources, but to transform wealth into justice, freedom, and repair. We are in the early stages of a new era of philanthropy—one that is meeting the challenges of our times by boldly imagining a future beyond extractive capitalism, white supremacy, colonialism, and patriarchy. In these consequential times, philanthropy must evolve our purpose from gilding—lightly covering up systemic challenges—to alchemy—investing in a true transformation of these systems.

The term *alchemy* has scientific, mythical, and philosophical roots and evokes early alchemists who attempted to transform base metals into gold. It is a metaphor that speaks to something experienced grantmakers know: Philanthropy is neither an art nor a science. True durable impact doesn't come from a check; it comes from an ever-evolving mix of relationships, resources, imagination, trust, and solidarity.

The "gold" we seek to create is a fair economy that works for all communities, a planet that can sustain generations to come, the repair of generations of harm, and the cultivation of a multiracial democracy where communities can shape the decisions that impact them. The "metal" of our time is the trillions in excess wealth, resources that could be used today for the public good, but instead remain locked away in endowments and donor-advised funds. Transformation is philanthropy's mandate in our times.

Many of us are clear-eyed that gilded philanthropy gets it wrong. But I want us to ask the question that Dr. Ayana Elizabeth Johnson, a writer, advocate, and marine biologist, brilliantly asks in her book by the same name, "What if we get it right?"[18] This question brings us back to the choice and agency we have and reminds us that it is what we do next that will determine the future.

What if we get it right? We have glimpses of what this will look like. A new era is boldly starting to take form, with reimagined practices, purposes, identities, norms, and impact:

- In 2024, after years of organizing led by Indigenous women, the oldest sacred shell mound site in California was rematriated and returned to its original people, the Confederated Villages of Lisjan Nation. A $20 million grant from a private foundation provided essential support to efforts to reclaim ancestral lands.

- A nonprofit is the only legal services provider for their clients, the majority of whom are low-income. After a revolving door of donors, one donor stays and offers a different kind of partnership: seven years of unrestricted support. The nonprofit's executive director can end the hiring and salary adjustment freeze and pay her staff and herself fairly. New leave and sabbatical policies are drafted. There is time for rest, for dreaming and planning. Community members are championed by lawyers who are well resourced to protect their rights.

- In the wake of the murder of George Floyd and the racial justice uprisings, a foundation leader brings together twelve funding partners to make large long-term flexible grants to organizations supporting the self-determined priorities of Black communities. Grantmaking is determined by an advisory group of women-of-color leaders with decades of experience in social and racial justice movements. The fund's goal is to achieve real democracy by investing in those most systematically excluded from it. Grantees and donors forge a new way of being in relationship with each other—with funders learning from those who are most impacted by injustice and coming away changed by the process.

- A sixty-year-old foundation decides to redistribute all their assets to social justice organizations. A trustee, who is also a community leader, describes it as the "time to compost" the institution. The foundation understands that it is the community, not the foundation, that should decide how this capital will best shape their future and meet their needs. Over the next five years, the foundation will redistribute their capital to communities through a series of experiments rooted in care and community self-determination.

- A family foundation drafting new governing bylaws gives movement leaders on the board the structural majority, ensuring that community voice will always determine how resources flow. As a result of this shift, longtime donors find themselves transformed, moving beyond the limited identity of "philanthropist" into new identities of cocreators and twenty-first century stewards. In these new roles, they relinquish control and forge relationships of partnership, building a shared future in which those who are proximate to communities have power and access to resources.

The past mingles with the future, inviting us to imagine and build anew. The question is not, Will the landscape of philanthropy change? (It has and will), but rather, How can we affirmatively transition philanthropy to meet the specific intersecting challenges of our times?

About Me

I bring to this book two decades of experience as a philanthropic practitioner. My first introduction to philanthropy was as a grantseeker. It is the lessons I learned then that have informed everything that's followed. As an activist in my early twenties, I connected with a group of young women who started the Third Wave Foundation. These women were at the forefront of social movements but felt invisible to mainstream philanthropy. So they set out to create a foundation designed to resource their peers. I joined them and for six years helped to build a philanthropy that was by and for our community. This experience became my DNA in philanthropy.

I was not born into wealth, though I have spent most of my career working to unlock resources for change—as an executive director of a private foundation, as a program officer and founding director of a collaborative fund, and as a board member of a public foundation. A lawyer by training, I bring attention and curiosity to the rules, stories, and governance that shape philanthropic practice.

I am also a daughter, mother, partner, and friend. I am an immigrant and the child of a refugee, shaped by the places I've called home: Houston, Brooklyn, and the Bay Area. I am of the many communities I belong to, and I am always at home with people who dream of a more just world and are working to make it so, in different ways, roles, and capacities. Of particular relevance to this book is the community of leaders I belong to, many of whom are women of color, who have been forging a new era of philanthropy and bringing about a sea change in how the sector works and understands itself. We engage in this alchemy of transforming wealth, experimenting with the resources of time and strategy, learning together, and seeding breakthroughs.

Leading in these years of overlapping crises has brought clarity of purpose and ample opportunities to experiment with funding practices rooted in trust, care, and solidarity. From New York to New Mexico, the West, and the Midwest, from the earliest days of the trust-based philanthropy movement to the vibrant forward-leaning donor community at the Solidaire Network, I have found fellow travelers in every corner of the sector. These years have brought me into deep listening with community leaders about where philanthropy falls short, and catalyzing cocreation with so many philanthropic colleagues to resource the future we need.

As a student of social change, I am constantly learning and am skeptical of easy answers and quick fixes, especially when it comes to transforming long-standing systems of injustice. Dreamers, makers, healers, and poets are my people. Creativity, care, and imagination are critical to my own life and practice, and I believe we can benefit from so much more of all these elements in philanthropy.

Practices for Our Times

My first choice for how we resource a more just future would be an effective and moral tax system that has the wealthiest paying their share, as well as a democratically elected government making decisions about resource allocation. But we must start with where we are, and reimagine the old infrastructures of wealth to resource this more-just future.

There is a narrative that change in philanthropy comes from the largest institutions and the best-known leaders. In my experience, change in the philanthropic sector, like in society, comes from the ground up: from program officers who listen deeply to grantees and shift their practice accordingly; from grants managers and chief financial officers using their power and tools to advance the mission; from trustees and foundation leaders who evolve their institutions to meet the moment, not because of how they will be perceived, but because they understand that we each have an important role to play; from grantseekers who courageously ask funders to demonstrate their trust with long-term capacity and support and speak out when funders abuse power. These shifts are coming together in a new era of philanthropy, and the stories in this book honor the work of the many people who are dreaming of and practicing transformational philanthropy.

Practice is how we evolve. To achieve transformative outcomes, we must imagine new stories, embrace proximate and accountable governance, leave behind relics of practice that speak to bygone eras, and adopt strategy and evaluation approaches that are emergent and values-aligned. We must invest our resources in the future we want and understand that transformation includes us too. Finally, we must leave behind a philanthropy that has played a role in creating a cult of an individual hero or savior and find greater power in collective ways of giving for our shared future.

I have a very imperfect yoga practice that I credit with teaching me a lot, including the meaning and value of practice. On the mat, I've learned that the big changes we seek (like a handstand!) come about by the small, consistent steps we take. Change is sometimes barely perceptible until one day it is a full-on breakthrough. To achieve the breakthrough, we return to the mat and work with what is there and present. Big shifts rarely happen on the first try. Yet with consistent and purposeful effort, we get there.

How to Read This Book

Throughout this book, you will hear stories, perspectives, and insights from trailblazers who are already building the next era of philanthropy. I hope you will join them in reflection and action.

The book is organized into ten chapters, each focusing on an aspect of philanthropic practice. The themes weaving through the practices include the progress created when we value imagination and experimentation; the impact we find when we evolve how we hold power; the magic that comes from living in interdependence, mutuality, and solidarity; and the possibilities we unleash when we shift into collective purpose and action.

I invite you to read this book in the fashion that best suits your purpose. Each chapter builds on the next but can also be read independently. You may be at the start of your philanthropic journey; if so, you can use this book to think about how you want to be part of building this new era. Some chapters are written with a primary audience in mind. For example, chapters on governance and investments may appeal to trustees and CFOs, whereas chapters addressing grants practice may be of greater interest to program officers. Each chapter includes practice prompts that you can use to put the learning into action. These practices highlight the importance of each role, from grantseeker to grantmaker, and how we can all evolve our practices in support of true transformation.

I have tried to balance this book with what I, and we, are learning together: the questions we must grapple with, and the creativity and hope required for the journey. While creating this book, my mantra was to write for the joy of it (not that it was all joyful!). I hope this fullness comes through. These times are serious; so is our work. And when we bring joy and lightness to it, it helps us move and move together.

I am grateful you are here. Together we can meet this moment and make possible the work of transforming wealth into a world where everyone has dignity and what they need to thrive. This book is a conversation, one that I hope you will continue long after you reach the end of these pages.

PRACTICE

1

Write a New Story

This chapter explores how our personal stories, institutional stories, and collective narratives merge to form an architecture that shapes our practice of philanthropy. As we excavate the multiple stories and narratives we hold and how they have formed us, we can ask: In these high-stakes times, what new stories do we need to boldly resource a more just and sustainable future?

> *We are the stories we are told and we are the stories we tell ourselves.*
>
> —HAROLD JOHNSON[1]

My practice of philanthropy has been shaped by stories.

One was seldom spoken and yet found its way to me in countless other ways. It is the story of my father, who was seven years old when his family stored their most precious belongings in a locker and left their home in the middle of the night, believing they would return a few weeks later.

My father's family joined fifteen million people in the largest forced migration in history, a result of Britain's partition of India into two countries, Muslim-majority Pakistan and Hindu-majority India. Somewhere between one and two million people lost their lives in the unspeakable violence that broke out.[2] My father's family, Hindus from the Sindh region, reached India physically intact. They spent time in refugee camps before reaching Mumbai, where my father's seven siblings worked so that he could go to school and raise his family out of poverty. As they rebuilt their lives in Mumbai, they experienced hardships, hunger, and precarity.

My father told me this story about staying up late at night as a teen to listen to a radio program that played Western music—he loved the Beatles and longed for the worlds he heard about in those songs. Those songs planted the seeds of his dream to leave India for the United States.

That dream came true when he was accepted into the Cooper Union for the Advancement of Science and Art in New York City to complete his master's degree in engineering. The Cooper Union provided a full scholarship to all admitted students, and my father worked for a year to save for a plane ticket. Eventually, he would sponsor his siblings and their children, and generations of our family would come to the United States. They would go on to achieve a prosperity that would have been inconceivable to our family who spent nights hungry in Mumbai.

My father's early experience of forced migration and poverty deeply shaped him. The scarcity of his childhood never felt far. His childhood trauma manifested in adulthood as mental health struggles, and money was a constant trigger. No matter how financially secure he was as an adult, he lived in fear of losing everything and returning to the struggles of his childhood. His relationship to money and resources was one of control.

I grew up reading newspapers with my dad, and we always talked about what was happening in the world at our dinner table. There is a particular kind of love that immigrants have for their adopted country, and my father was no exception. In me, he instilled the idea that a democracy only works when each of us meets our responsibility to be informed and engaged. There were no easy answers, but there was always a duty to grapple, engage, and contribute.

When he passed away a few years ago, I tried to put together the puzzle pieces of his life, and in the process, I found pieces of me. I hold two, and maybe more, of these pieces in my philanthropic practice. In uncertain times like the one we are living through, I find that my body has a memory, passed down to me, about the dangers of rising authoritarianism, escalating hate, and what it means for people's lives when they don't have the power to make decisions about their fates. I also notice my acute sensitivity to how money can be a tool for control, and my desire to reimagine resourcing relationships to be rooted in trust.

———

My mother's story dramatically differs from my father's. It is her life that has shaped mine the most. My mother's family was also from Sindh but had moved before 1947. My grandfather started a successful business and was able to help many Sindhi families arriving in India during the Partition, connecting them with jobs and resources.

A thread of plenty runs through my mother's childhood stories. She shares a story from her childhood that I love: The family of seven brothers and sisters would pile into a car and drive out of the city into the countryside, to groves of mango trees. They would choose a tree and hire a local worker to climb up and pick all the ripe mangoes on it. Even now, my mother's eyes sparkle as she describes it. "Dimple, there were hundreds of mangoes!" With joy, she recounts how they would go home with a car full of mangoes, delighting in the abundance.

My mom's childhood was stable and materially comfortable, but in adulthood, she navigated hardships. Like too many women of her generation, my mother did not have a say in who she married. Deep-seated cultural narratives about gender played out as my mother spent two decades in a marriage that she did not choose. Yet, within the choices that she could make, she always chose to throw herself into care, community, and helping others.

My mom's experience of leaving behind everyone she loved to move to the United States for an arranged marriage was isolating. She wanted to spare others the loneliness of her own experience, so our home was always full of people starting their lives in this country. Even today, when someone in our family or community needs something, my mom is usually the first person they call.

My mother's relationship with money and resources is of trust and generosity. I never heard the word *philanthropy* growing up, but I saw my mom embody this truth: When we lean into care, there is always enough. My mother's story shapes my understanding of philanthropy as being how we use and share our collective resources to care for each other. Across cultures and generations, and long before the advent of institutional funding, this is what philanthropy has been: how we each contribute what we have to take care of each other and grow our collective well-being. We see this idea of philanthropy live on today in feminist approaches to funding, in mutual aid, and in giving circles.

Money Stories

The stories we carry shape us, our actions, our imaginations, our understanding of what is possible. Movement leaders that I deeply respect have taught me about the importance of lineage, and I share these stories as offerings of my lineage.

My stories live in me; their imprint can be found in my work resourcing social change. These stories have given me a sensitivity to power dynamics and differentials and helped me build relationships rooted in care and mutuality. My father's fear of scarcity haunted me in my early days as a program officer. I struggled to "give away" a grant's budget in its entirety, always holding some funds back, afraid of a future lack.

Over the years, as my practice deepened, I've drawn on my mother's ability to create abundance by centering care in my work. Some of the smallest grants I've made have been transformative beyond their size because of the purpose, intent, and relationship behind them.

In 2018, a little over a year into the first Trump administration, when our grantees at General Service Foundation (GSF) began showing signs of burnout and exhaustion, we responded with flexible wellness grants as additions to our core support. These grants were specifically intended for the wellness, sustainability, safety, and joy of the staff of our grantees. They were modest ten-thousand-dollar grants, on top of grants that were a hundred thousand dollars or more, and yet, grantees shared that these dedicated funds for their wellness made them feel seen and cared for. Recipients told us it wasn't the size of the grant that mattered, but the message of care and the conversations it surfaced on their teams that made the difference.

One recipient organization was working with families that had been forcibly separated from their children at the US-Mexico border. The grant inspired organizational leaders to have a conversation with staff about what they needed for their personal well-being. Staff shared the deep sadness and trauma they were holding from accompanying families navigating the nightmare of separation from their children. Our grant supported a mix of mental health resources for staff and gestures to spark joy and community, including a dinner on the beach and surprise gift cards.

This same inquiry at another organization revealed that staff who were working from home in a time of escalating Islamophobia feared for their safety and the safety of their families. That organization used our grants to purchase doorbells with security cameras for each staff member. I will never forget when a colleague shared that she and her staff slept better because of our wellness grant.

Today, more funders are recognizing wellness and safety as growing needs. Thankfully, they are making similar investments. While our core grants were flexible, grantees rarely felt they could use grant dollars to care for themselves and their staff. This is the reality of philanthropic culture. These small grants went against that grain and said to grantees, *You matter, and we want you, who are doing such important work, to be well and thriving.*

Fund Us Like You Want Us to Win

Ash-Lee Henderson, co-executive director of the Highlander Center, reminds funders that they should "fund us like you want us to win." My own experience of the connection between resources and progress has shaped my funding philosophy and has helped me understand what Ash-Lee means when she says this. I learned the connection between resources and winning during my first two years of lawyering.

I spent my first year after law school at a large New York City law firm (think the TV series *Suits* on Netflix). It was 2002, the economy was in recession, and I was assigned to a prominent bankruptcy case where our purpose was to help a lender get back their loan. The firm invested in our capacity to win, provided us with weeks of rigorous onboarding and training, and then mentorship and supervision to help us grow our skills as lawyers. The ethos of the practice was clear: Give our everything to every case. We had large teams and access to every kind of support so we could win each and every case. If we could imagine a resource that would help us win, that resource was ours to use.

I left the law firm after a year, excited to put my training to use and tip the scales of justice in favor of those shut out of power. I accepted a position at South Brooklyn Legal Services representing low-income New Yorkers who could not afford a lawyer. My clients were navigating a harrowing mix of losses, including loss of shelter, access to food, employment, and even the heartbreaking loss of custody of their children. My salary was about 25 percent of what I made at the law firm, and I went from working on one or two cases at one time to having a caseload of forty clients at any given time. Why so many clients? Our funders wanted us to serve as many clients as possible, and someone had assessed that this was the greatest number of people we could technically serve with our limited resources. The goal was no longer winning the absolute most we could for every client; the resources simply didn't allow for it. Rather, we were just trying to help our clients survive. The message this time was: Don't imagine resources you might need to win, because we don't have access to them.

The contrast of working in the same profession and capacity but in these polar-opposite contexts taught me a lesson about the centrality of resources and who is seen as deserving of resources. The resources that we have influence not only whether we win or lose, but what we can imagine, and what our work feels like. To be clear, resources are not the sole factor. But without abundant resources, winning is much harder.

I have seen this as a funder over the last two decades. When we fund with little dribs and drabs of resources, we see little dribs and drabs of change. If we resource a just future abundantly, we will give people what they need to win and create a world where we all can flourish and thrive.

Importantly, I don't mean financial resources alone. I am referring to everything we can bring to bear as funders: imagination, community, connections, knowledge, investments in infrastructure and capacity, partnership, and solidarity.

Institutional Stories and Donor Stories

Experts on narrative change have long emphasized the importance of stories, and how our shared stories shape our beliefs, our interpretations, our collective sense of boundaries, and the possibilities we hold. Philanthropy is also shaped by institutional stories and shared sector stories. Examining what they are and how they influence our practice is a critical first step in imagining how we collectively write a new story.

Donors and organizations have deeply embedded narratives that drive and shape their work. For many foundations, the story of their founding donor's life, passions, and wishes becomes a guiding story. There is the powerful story of "donor intent" that carries with it legal power and consequences. In philanthropic circles, people commonly note how institutional cultures carry the stamp of how a founder made their money. For example, a foundation funded through venture capital may have a culture of risk-taking. Other narratives live in organizations, sometimes spoken aloud but often in the background, shaping relationships and possibilities.

While philanthropy has changed and evolved over the last century, too many of our stories have remained the same. These stories justify a set of norms, behaviors, and ways of operating and reinforce the idea that this is how things are and will always be.

Here are four common powerful institutional stories that shape our work. Although these stories are familiar, it is important to remember that they can also change.

1. "It's My Money"

Within philanthropic institutions, a story of "It's my money" profoundly shapes how power operates in our work. The implication is, "Therefore I can do (or not do) whatever I want." It isn't that these words are often spoken out loud, though I have heard them said. Rather, they are infused in our practices and our organizational cultures.

When Andrew Carnegie dictated that his design preferences should overrule community needs for the thousands of libraries he built, he embodied the "It's my money" story. But this gilded philanthropy story wasn't left in Carnegie's time. We see it in today's headlines when donors use their power to object to university hires or want to see their names on the hospital wings they've supported.[3]

The "It's my money" story obscures the fact that when resources are put into an endowment or a donor-advised fund, they cease to belong to the donor. Today donors receive a tax benefit in exchange for putting this money toward public purposes. In the United States, in 2022 taxpayers lost out on $73.24 billion that could have gone into the public coffers as taxes but was instead given to donors as subsidies for charitable giving.[4]

But this story is less about who technically owns the money and more about who should decide its use. In practice, the "It's my money" story centers donors as decision-makers, creating a constant loop of labor on the part of grantseekers: days spent preparing for site visits, presentations, and compiling evaluation metrics. This labor focuses on the donor and the belief that the money is theirs and that they alone should get to decide how to put it to public use.

2. "You Do You": A Story About Individuality

I recently spoke on a panel along with a philanthropic colleague, Chloe Cockburn, who has a beautiful practice of sharing her strategy memos on criminal justice reform funding with an email list of hundreds of funders. Over the years, I have read her memos to learn from her thinking and reflections in real time. I complimented her generosity and lifted her practice as an example of how our sector can work more collectively. Several people in the audience had also been reading her memos and they echoed my gratitude. She thanked us, and then shared what, to me, is a classic philanthropy story.

In all her years of sharing her memos, she rarely had anyone disagree with something she shared. Her messages always included a sentence inviting readers to share feedback and comments. She included this line with the hope that people would respond, and if they disagreed, help push her thinking.

I wasn't surprised that no one had reached out to share disagreement with her because one of philanthropy's stories is, "You do you." It is a story about individuality and each donor's "freedom" to do anything they want to do. In this story, each foundation has their own assessment of a challenge, and their own solutions, with funders failing to see themselves as part of a collective. If we happen to share an analysis, that opens room for collaboration, but we don't assume that a shared analysis is the goal. We definitely don't assume that we have the right to tell another foundation, or its staff, what they can do, think, or fund. The "You do you" story speaks to an individualized and atomized way of understanding our work, one that dramatically limits our sector's impact.

3. "Our Funding Is a Mere Drop in the Bucket"

It is never easy to make funding cuts, and trustees rarely make decisions to pull back. And yet, when foundations reduce their funding commitments, they often justify it by telling themselves that their funding is a "mere drop in the bucket." At first glance, the drop-in-the-bucket story sounds like a story about humility, but in reality this narrative encourages us to keep our hopes and ambitions small. In organizations, it is a story that tends to come up in moments of retraction, when we are cutting grant budgets and don't want to feel bad. We say "our funding is a mere drop in the bucket" because we don't want to grapple with the harm that will come from us not doing our part.

In a sector that cumulatively has $1.6 trillion in assets, foundations big and small often share a story about how insignificant their funding is relative to any particular challenge. We also tell ourselves this story to explain why we aren't doing the most we can possibly do.

This was a story that numerous foundation boards told in the early months of the pandemic when their assets initially dropped but the needs had grown greater. Some foundations increased their funding while others compared themselves to drops. The natural extension of this story is: Even if we were all in, it would never be enough.

4. "To Whom Much Is Given, Much Is Expected"

This take on the Bible verse Luke 12:48 asserts that the most fortunate have a responsibility and duty that accompanies their good fortune. For many donors, this is the "why" of their philanthropy. This narrative ties the responsibility to give, care, and contribute to one's financial fortune and privilege. Another layer to this story is that Carnegie and his peers believed that the wealthiest were wealthy because they were the smartest and fittest and that their duty to look after the poor was rooted in the poor being less able to make good decisions.[5] This is a terrible story. It tells us that we are engaged in philanthropy not because it is the moral response to extreme inequality, but rather because we are fortunate, and we are fortunate because we are better than the less fortunate.

How might our practice of philanthropy shift with a story that is not centered on our good fortune and superiority but rather one of transformational solidarity across class and race? What if our primary story was about how our freedoms are inextricably linked to those of others? A story of interdependence, relationship, and mutuality rather than exception and responsibility. A story that says we all deserve to flourish, that we are bound to each other? As Fannie Lou Hamer said, "Nobody's free until everybody's free,"[6] and *that* is the "why" of our work.

Philanthropy's Scarcity Story

The stories we tell, individually and institutionally, like the four stories above, contribute to a larger narrative of philanthropy. When these stories are repeated without deeper examination or understanding, they become the de facto basis that funders operate from.

The most pervasive story in the philanthropic sector is the story of scarcity. This is the story we tell about how our resources are not enough. This "not enough" story shapes our philanthropic practices, relationships, strategies, and, most importantly, in this moment, our understanding of what is possible. We see this in action when markets go down and foundations reduce grants budgets despite having millions or billions in their endowments. We see it when funders try to "solve problems" in proportion to their own scale, not in proportion to the actual needs and what can be achieved collectively in partnership with communities, other funders, and government. We see it in a host of relational dynamics between funders and the field that foment competition and lead to burnout.

"Not enough" is more than a story. Even in the most resourced part of the social sector, "not enough" is a surprisingly common feeling. Communities and fundraisers often have experiences with funders that leave them feeling like what they are doing is not enough, that they themselves are not enough.

As we think about the stories that shape us, it is helpful to remember that the story of not enough is not just a philanthropic narrative. It is also a core narrative of capitalism. Philanthropy is a child of the specific form of capitalism that we live in that has both produced extreme inequality and has put funders in positions of power over trillions of dollars of private capital stored away in endowments for public purposes. The scarcity story is one of philanthropy's origin stories and part of the sector's lineage. The philanthropic norms that flow from the scarcity story impede impact at every turn.

With trillions of dollars held in the sector for public purposes, how do we so often operate from a place of lack? The scarcity story isn't just flawed with respect to the amount of resources we have: Scarcity keeps us from seeing, understanding, and owning the true fullness of the resources available for supporting change. There are trillions in capital, yes, and also so much more. Capital is but one of the resources we as funders deploy for social change. We can also resource change with imagination, community, knowledge, and relationship. All these things can exist in plenty when we are willing to see and use them.

Abundance: A New Story for These Times

It's time that we write a new story and forge new ways of being during this new and most consequential era of philanthropy's work. In times of high stakes, we can't afford to embody scarcity. We must shift toward a practice that embodies abundance, that says unequivocally that we have what we need to meet this moment. We have enough, and importantly, we are enough, and you, our partners in building the world we need, are more than enough.

In practice, this story invites us to imagine what we might do if we believed we could meet this moment. Abundance invites us to see how unlocking our collective resources is a fundamental part of how we make a world in which we all thrive. We begin to see how our resources are bigger than just the funding in our portfolio or institution. We understand that we belong to a broader network and that the resources we are all deploying toward a more just future include capital, relationships, imagination, knowledge, and more. In the abundance story, the possibilities are collective, and we begin to see ourselves as part of an ecosystem in which we evolve together. As stewards of philanthropic resources in this new era, we realize that our role is to transform wealth into new possibilities and futures.

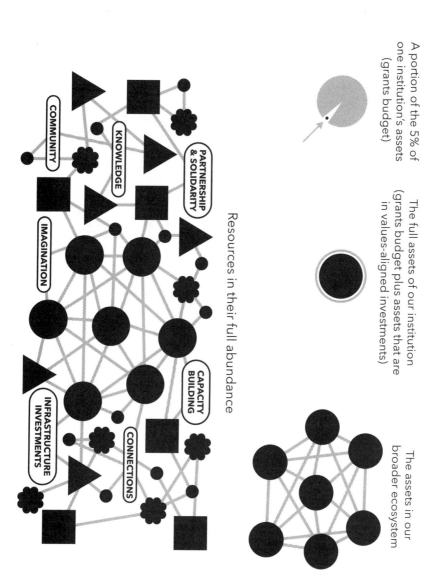

The Resources That Philanthropy Can Deploy Toward a More Just and Sustainable Future

A portion of the 5% of one institution's assets (grants budget)

The full assets of our institution (grants budget plus assets that are in values-aligned investments)

The assets in our broader ecosystem

Resources in their full abundance

COMMUNITY

KNOWLEDGE

PARTNERSHIP & SOLIDARITY

IMAGINATION

CAPACITY BUILDING

INFRASTRUCTURE INVESTMENTS

CONNECTIONS

PRACTICE PROMPTS

Story Circle

1. Place chairs in a circle and invite your team to take a seat.

2. Each participant shares a story about their relationship to money, reflecting on how the stories shape their fundraising or grantmaking work.

3. After participants have shared their stories, have a group reflection on themes and throughlines.

Abundance Vision Board

1. Assemble art supplies, including magazines, scissors, markers, and other materials that can be used for making vision boards.

2. With a group or on your own, create a vision board that represents abundance to you.

3. If you do this activity with a group, create a gallery of the vision boards.

4. Close out the activity with a discussion about what would shift in your work if you believed you had what you need to meet this moment.

Know Your History, So You Can Build the Future

Today's philanthropy originates from the Gilded Age, a time like ours when extreme social inequality posed a threat to democracy. Nearly 140 years have passed since Andrew Carnegie published *The Gospel of Wealth*, yet its ideas profoundly shape today's philanthropic purpose and practice. This chapter brings us into conversation with Carnegie, examining the roots of modern philanthropy to understand how we got here, and what we must change to meet the challenges of our times.

The conversation employs original questions from me and answers from Carnegie that quote his Gospel of Wealth.

Philanthropy, Then and Now

The New Era of Philanthropy Podcast

Transcript: Dimple Abichandani interviews Andrew Carnegie

[Music playing]

DIMPLE ABICHANDANI: Welcome to the *New Era of Philanthropy* podcast, where we reimagine how wealth can be transformed into a more just and sustainable future. I'm your host, Dimple Abichandani.

[Music fades out]

Thank you for tuning in. Listeners, today we talk with our guest Andrew Carnegie, hailed as the "father of modern philanthropy" about his seminal *Gospel of Wealth*.

An American Experience PBS biography notes that Carnegie "saw himself as a hero of working people, yet he crushed their unions. One of the most successful entrepreneurs of his age, he railed against privilege. A generous philanthropist, he slashed the wages of the workers who made him rich."[1] We are going to talk with Andrew about how these contradictions are alive in *The Gospel of Wealth* and the vision for philanthropy he put forth in 1889.

Carnegie's *Gospel of Wealth* provides instructions for what people with excess wealth should do in an increasingly unequal world. I will give you a sneak preview: Andrew envisioned a philanthropy that treats the harms caused by unjust systems while leaving those systems in place.

It's a juicy conversation, listeners, and I am glad you are here!

[Music playing]

Welcome to the podcast, Andrew Carnegie! Thank you for taking the time to speak with us. First, a confession. Andrew, I worked in philanthropy for almost two decades before I read *The Gospel of Wealth*. When I finally did read your essays, I couldn't shake the feeling of having stumbled onto the Rosetta Stone of the philanthropic sector. I knew that we needed to have this conversation with you.

So let me fill in our audience. You wrote these two essays in 1889 to an audience of your fellow millionaires. You might be interested to learn that even today *The Gospel of Wealth* still finds its way to millionaires, and now billionaires, often given to them by wealth and philanthropic advisers. Warren Buffet gifted your essays to a young Bill Gates.[2]

You begin your essays by grounding us in the rapid changes occurring in your times. Today we find ourselves, again, in another moment of tumult and transition, in the early years of a new era of philanthropy.

Andrew, what inspired you to write *The Gospel of Wealth*?

ANDREW CARNEGIE: *The problem of our age is the proper administration of wealth, so that the ties of brotherhood may still bind together the rich and poor in harmonious relationship.*[3]

DA: So, you were longing for a harmonious relationship between the rich and the poor, and you hoped that philanthropy could inspire that. I also long to live in a society with deeper cohesiveness, harmony, and care, a society in which people have what they need to thrive. Since you wrote *The Gospel of Wealth,* philanthropy has grown dramatically, with close to 120,000 foundations in the United States today and many more private donors and donors outside of formal institutions.[4]

And yet, that harmony you desired remains elusive. Today we've got deep polarization, fractured civic relationships, and accelerated inequality. As for philanthropy, I'm sorry to tell you that its intended beneficiaries often experience it as a tool for power and control rather than harmony and care.

Tell me more about the central question you're trying to answer in *The Gospel of Wealth.*

AC: *What is the proper mode of administering wealth after the laws upon which civilization is founded have thrown it into the hands of the few? It is of this great question that I believe I offer the true solution.*

DA: Of course I want to hear more about this "true solution," but wow—I'm stuck on your use of the phrase "laws of civilization" to refer to capitalism. In your essay you acknowledge that the same economic system that allowed you and a handful of your contemporaries to amass unheard-of fortunes inflicted incredible harm and struggle to the lives of the majority. And yet, you passionately argue that this system is best, saying, *"We accept and welcome therefore, as conditions to which we must accommodate ourselves, great inequality of environment; the concentration of business, industrial and commercial, in the hands of a few; and the law of competition between these, as being not only beneficial, but essential for the future progress of the race."*

I've got to tell you Andrew, almost 140 years later, the crisis of inequality has only deepened. The rules of our economy benefit the wealthiest, driving extreme concentration of wealth. Between 2020 and 2023, the richest five men in the world doubled their fortunes.[5] During that same time, almost five billion people globally have become poorer.[6]

Moreover, the capitalism you celebrate is, and always has been, racialized. US Federal Reserve data in 2019 finds that "the typical white family has eight times the wealth of the typical Black family, and five times the wealth of the typical Hispanic family."[7] "Past and present discrimination in critical markets—including housing, banking, taxation, higher education, and more"[8]—have compounded a racial wealth gap, with inequality deepening through the generations in the absence of disruptive forces.

In this new era of philanthropy, our starting point radically departs from yours: Our purpose must be to transform the systems of how wealth and power are administered so that they can be shared more equitably. In this new era, we are reaching out across class to dream of and invest in an economy that produces flourishing for all.

But please, go on. You were talking about the "true solution" you see to the problem of too much wealth in the hands of the few? I am eager to hear more about this vision for philanthropy.

AC: *We shall have an ideal state in which surplus wealth of the few will become, in the best sense, the property of the many, because administered for the common good, and this wealth, passing through the hands of the few, can be made a much more potent force for the elevation of our race than if it had been distributed in small sums to the people themselves.*

DA: OK, so about half of what you just said resonates, and the other half raises big red flags.

The idea that philanthropy should be used as a vehicle for moving excess money to become the "property of many" sounds really good. I love that you are talking about the "common good." On this podcast we are big fans of the common good.

Now the red flags. You are using the words "small sums" to refer to wages. You are saying that it is better for people that their wages be small and that the wealthy tend to their needs through philanthropy. This is a troubling statement that exposes a truth—that excess wealth is often the result of exploitation and extraction. In your example, it was the failure to pay living wages. Where this is the case, philanthropy is a false story, a decoy, a distraction from the true solutions that will bring about justice.

I'm also hearing lots of assumptions about the role of a donor.

AC: *The man of wealth . . . is best calculated to produce the most beneficial results for the community—the man of wealth thus becoming the mere agent and trustee for his poorer brethren, bringing to their service his superior wisdom, experience, and ability to administer, doing for them better than they would or could do for themselves.*

DA: Hmm. The "superior wisdom" of this man of wealth, why does this sound so familiar?

Ah—this is where the idea of "funders know best" came from! Your vision of donors "administering wealth" for the community better than it could or would have done for itself became the blueprint for generations of philanthropic culture and practice.

Ok, so let me catch you up, Andrew. While your idea about donors' "superior wisdom" still infuses too many philanthropic cultures, this gilded philanthropy "billionaires know best" approach doesn't make sense in our times, especially because the billionaires have played a central role in creating the challenges we face. Today, we understand that those closest to the challenges have the deepest understanding of the needed solutions. To grasp the nuances of how oppressive systems are created, experienced, and solved for, Bryan Stevenson, founder of the Equal Justice Initiative and author of *Just Mercy*, urges us to "get proximate to people who are suffering."[9] We understand today that when philanthropy assumes this mantle of superiority, not only are we not achieving our goals, we are likely causing harm. In this new era, philanthropic practitioners engage in participatory and trust-based approaches that move resources, decision-making, and power back to communities.

OK, Andrew, let's end our conversation with the most important topic: purpose. Tell me how you thought about philanthropy's purpose in your times.

AC: *Our duty is with what is practicable now; with the next step possible in our day and generation. It is criminal to waste our energies in endeavoring to uproot, when all we can profitably or possibly accomplish is to bend the universal tree of humanity a little in the direction most favorable to the production of good fruit under existing circumstances.*

DA: This question of purpose is at the heart of where philanthropy's past and future must part.

You are describing a gilded philanthropy that leaves harmful systems in place and tries to do a little good around the edges. Today, a growing community of funders understands philanthropy's mandate in our consequential times as uprooting unjust systems and transforming them into systems that contribute to everyone's flourishing.

Your vision of "bending a little" has borne out in a sector that approaches its purpose of resourcing, with "little" amounts, on average spending 5 percent of their corpus annually.[10]

Bending the universal tree of humanity "a little" reminds me of a debate at the family foundation I led. The founding donor had penned a wise letter about his "hopes that through this medium [the foundation] some good would be done for humanity."[11] Later in the letter, he refers to his hope for the "most good."

The use of two different phrases—"some good" and "most good"— set up a debate about the founder's true intent, with the difference between the two being significant. The "some good" approach is a foundation doing the legally required minimum: spending 5 percent of its endowment, filing the required tax disclosures, and so on. The "most good" approach raises the bar and inspires us to think about all the ways that we as funders could meet the moment, transform conditions, and transform ourselves in the process.

Another way we can think about purpose is to ask who should benefit the most from philanthropy. Too often, philanthropy's benefits go to the philanthropists. Philanthropy is seen as an identity, a hobby, a way to avoid taxes, a business strategy, or a way to keep family connections going through future generations.

Andrew, here is an example of the benefits of philanthropy flowing to the philanthropist: Today we know the Ford Foundation as one of the largest and most impactful social justice funders, with a clear purpose of solving inequality in its many forms.

But as was reported in the *New York Times,* "In setting up the [Ford] Foundation, Henry Ford's principal wish was to avert any public ownership of FMC (Ford Motor Company), and at the same time to ensure that after he died, his family would retain control of the company. He was successful on both counts. If Henry Sr. had died without creating the Foundation, his heirs would have been saddled with estate taxes of over $300 million. To pay those taxes, they almost certainly would have had to sell some Ford stock to outsiders."[12]

It gets worse! Henry Ford required the Ford Foundation to pay taxes incurred by his heirs, and the foundation "did ultimately pay inheritance taxes of $55,370,068."[13] I'd love to say that this was old news or an exception, but even today, websites offering philanthropic services highlight the tax benefits, and wealthy donors at conferences talk about philanthropy as a strategy for family cohesion.

Tax schemes, business experiments, family reunions—it's hard to argue that any of these are a "public purpose" or an appropriate use of funds held in the public trust. In this new era of philanthropy, we are imagining a philanthropy in which philanthropists are not the key beneficiaries. As we grapple with this legacy of philanthropy's first 140 years, we can see why we've landed where we are today and the urgency of updating our purpose if we want to meet the challenges of our times.

We are running out of time, and we didn't get to ask you what you are reading these days, so we will have to have you back on the show. Thank you, Andrew, for joining us!

Here is what I am taking away from our conversation: The philanthropy we've known—that you envisioned—was never about changing the systems that create and fuel inequality. Philanthropy's next chapter, this new era that so many of us are forging, must commit not just to lessening harms but to transforming the systems that cause inequality in the first place. I leave our conversation understanding that we must leave your blueprint in the past and build a new one for this era. I see all around us, amazing practitioners who are doing just that.

[Music]

[End of transcript]

The Best Fields for Philanthropy Then and Now

In his *Gospel of Wealth,* Carnegie offered a specific and influential list of the seven "best fields for philanthropy": universities, libraries, hospitals (and the prevention of human suffering), public parks, public spaces like concert halls and gathering places, swimming baths (pools), and churches, while making the case for why each is worthy of investment. This list still draws some of the largest donations today.

As we try to meet the urgent challenges and opportunities of our times, we need a new list of "best fields" to guide this next era of philanthropy. Here is my updated list of where philanthropic investment can make the greatest impact today. While I've structured the list in a fashion similar to Carnegie's list, this is not one donor's idea of what is best. Rather, this list is inspired by being a part of a growing community of funders who work in solidarity with community partners and are building a new era of philanthropy.

1. In Times of Rising Authoritarianism, Invest in the Building of a Multiracial Democracy

A healthy functioning democracy is a precondition to almost every other goal that funders may be working toward. With that understanding, every funder should see themselves as a democracy funder. Democracy is under attack around the world, with rising authoritarianism posing a threat in many countries. In the United States, we are living through a backsliding and devolving of rights, including voting rights and reproductive rights. While support for democracy funding has increased in recent years, it is still less than 1 percent of overall institutional giving.[14]

In advocating that philanthropy invest in strengthening our multiracial democracy, I don't want to gloss over the fraught relationship that philanthropy has with a healthy democracy. After all, many have rightly argued that philanthropy poses a threat to our democracy, as it concentrates wealth and power. A lack of transparency amplifies the risk of wealth and power being used in ways that tip the scales in favor of the interests of the wealthy.

But these aren't normal times. Entire communities have had their votes and voices suppressed. The dismantling of the Voting Rights Act, as well as legislative efforts to create barriers to voting, have fueled a racial turn-out gap. In 2023 alone, fourteen states enacted seventeen restrictive voting laws.[15] A Brennan Center study found that the nationwide difference in voting rates between white voters and voters of color has grown consistently since 2012. "In 2022, the racial turnout gap was 18 percentage points, meaning 14 million more ballots would have been cast" by voters of color that year were it not for efforts to suppress votes.[16]

Nonprofits championing multiracial democracy find themselves increasingly targeted with "threats to physical, digital, and personal safety, negative media characterizations, actual or threatened litigation, and reduction in funding."[17] Funders are also finding themselves the target of attacks and legal harassment for investing in our democracy. Philanthropic efforts aimed at addressing systemic inequities like the Fearless Fund, which made grants to Black women entrepreneurs, have been aggressively challenged.[18] These times call for funders to be courageous and to invest in the safety of leaders and organizations that are standing up and fighting for our democracy.

Democracy funding has sometimes been understood to be a narrow and technical field focused on voting, but I appreciate this vision for democracy offered by Deepak Bhargava, President of the JPB Foundation, of "democracy in the broader sense of people's ability to shape the direction of society and their communities."[19] Funders forging a new era of philanthropy understand that we resource a healthy democracy when we fund community organizing and people power, and we do so year-round, not just during election cycles.

2. Repair Harm

The desire for "harmonious relationships" is still a deep need today, and echoes through the years from Carnegie's time to our new era. A philanthropy that has the purpose of repair offers a pathway into a more just future and begins with acknowledging the harm that has been done. In this new era, funders can engage in reparative philanthropy as a powerful way to recognize how philanthropic capital often comes from extractive and exploitative practices.[20]

In the United States, one way that funders repair harm is through efforts to return stolen land to Indigenous communities. In 2024, the Sogorea Te' Land Trust secured the return of a Shellmound and Historic Village Site to the Lisjan Ohlone in West Berkeley—the result of yearslong advocacy and organizing.[21] The Kataly Foundation invested $20 million into this effort to return land to Indigenous stewardship, with the grant leveraging additional public funding from the city of Berkeley. "Philanthropy has a long history of extracting wealth from communities. Making this Shuumi contribution is one step toward repair, and it is also our responsibility as a foundation that exists on Ohlone land," said Nwamaka Agbo, CEO of the Kataly Foundation.[22] Increasingly, donors and foundations are partnering with land trusts and tribes who are purchasing back land that was stolen from them. These efforts are early, but I can imagine a time in the future when they will have taken hold.

Across the country, a multitude of reparations efforts are finally gaining ground at the city, state, and federal levels. Heather McGhee describes reparations as the "seed capital for the nation we are becoming."[23] Importantly, funders exploring reparations are not looking to philanthropy to bear the cost of reparations but to play a key role in supporting organizations that can create the conditions for reparations at the state and federal levels. Aria Florant, cofounder of Liberation Ventures, describes that she and her cofounder were "seeking the deepest-level root cause intervention on racial injustice," and this exploration led them to reparations.[24] Liberation Ventures invests in organizations advancing reparations and building a culture of repair that centers the healing, well-being, and safety of Black people. Aria notes that philanthropy also has an important role to play in modeling racial repair. "Funders can engage in courageous work to understand the history of their wealth, the ways the endowment has been invested over time, the grantmaking practices they have used, and if there has been harm, they can move through a cycle of racial repair."[25]

3. Build the New Infrastructures of Our Times

Carnegie transformed his wealth into the built infrastructures of his time—libraries, parks, universities, and event halls. Today's donors can invest in a different kind of infrastructure: not just the physical structures that organize our cities and communities, but the new frameworks that inform our values and determine how we move forward. How will we imagine and invest in new ways of understanding the economy, narrative infrastructure, and relational infrastructure that help us realize more just and sustainable ways of being? There is also the resiliency infrastructure that our times require. Almost every system we rely on will be tested as we go through this next period of change, whether it is due to climate change, the evolution of AI technology, or other elements of the polycrisis.

4. Shift Power and Invest in Power Building

In 2015, I was at the Funders' Committee for Civic Participation gathering when activist and author Alicia Garza addressed the room. "If you're funding civic engagement, and you're not doing it with a racial justice lens, aren't you just building the power of white voters?" Her words captured a reality that is not always understood by funders—that adding resources to weighted systems without trying to change who holds power only supercharges the inequitable status quo. Today, more funders understand that they must apply a power analysis to their work—including how race, gender, sexuality, ability, class, immigration status, and a range of other factors influence who has access to power. With that awareness comes the opportunity to invest in strategies that support communities in power building. The Building Movement Project defines power building as, "strategies for directly impacted communities to bring about change by reshaping systems and transforming material conditions."[26]

The depth of commitment funders bring to shifting power must be greater than the entrenched systems they seek to uproot. And those systems run deep. Strategies that shift power must be fundamental to the work of philanthropy—whether that work is focused on the arts, climate change, education, or any other issue.

Given that funders and grantees often have a different lived experience of power, it is important to have an understanding of power that is shaped by the lived experience of our grantees. Farhad Ebrahimi, founder and president of the Chorus Foundation, shares how Chorus Foundation partners, many of whom have historically had power wielded against them, talk about power today:

> Our grantees do not only talk about "climate solutions" or "climate justice." Today, they talk about a "just transition." We have seen climate organizations, including mainstream climate philanthropy, begin to address the need for "systems

change." But systems, as it turns out, change all the time, and "systemic change" can be dangerous if it doesn't center both equity and power. As we've learned from our friends at Movement Generation, "Transition is inevitable. Justice is not."[27]

5. Invest in Resilient Communities and a Sustainable Future

And speaking of climate justice: The urgency of the climate crisis has drawn billions in new funding. But only 1.3 percent of environmental funding goes to BIPOC-led climate justice organizations.[28] Too many climate funders have been slow to recognize and fund the environmental justice organizations that have long been on the front lines of fighting climate change. These organizations understand that climate solutions require people solutions.

In general, I would never say, "Be like Jeff Bezos," but I do love the story about what happened when he made a $10 billion commitment to climate funding through his Bezos Earth Fund. Bezos had the good sense to listen to the brilliant Gloria Walton, president and CEO of the Solutions Project, who shared with Bezos the distinction between where climate funding is most needed and most effective (grassroots organizing) and where it tends to go (large policy organizations and technocratic solutions).[29] Bezos responded with a $141 million commitment to four funding collaboratives—the Solutions Project, the Climate and Clean Energy Equity Fund, NDN Collective, and the Hive Fund for Climate and Gender Justice—which in turn fund grassroots climate organizations.[30] We should borrow this smart move and learn from leaders like Gloria Walton who have decades of experience in exactly the kind of grassroots organizing that we need to meet the challenges of climate change.

Marion Gee and Gloria Walton put out this call to funders:

> As climate justice funding flows from philanthropies and governments, there's a danger that it will be siphoned off by big, well-resourced, top-down organizations before it reaches frontline climate communities. Philanthropy has a responsibility to support the grassroots during this potential green gold

rush and to see that the flow of funding doesn't make inequities worse or weaken climate solutions.[31]

6. Accompaniment of Social Movements

We live in times marked by vibrant social movements for racial, gender, economic, disability, and climate justice. Think Standing Rock, Black Lives Matter, the Women's March, Not One More Deportation, as well as other smaller but equally impactful movements, like the Fight for 15. At times, funders have struggled with how they can productively relate to social movements. In this new era, funders engage in a philanthropy that *accompanies* the social movements that are dramatically changing what is possible.

What is accompaniment? The ideal of accompaniment was articulated by Archbishop Oscar Romero in El Salvador in the 1970s during a struggle for democracy. Believing that "despite the deep chasms between classes, the destinies of the rich and poor remain intertwined," Romero saw accompaniment as a metaphor for how "people from diverse backgrounds could come together in shared work, uniting around the needs and interests of the most oppressed."[32]

A gilded philanthropy has little interest in accompaniment because it does not acknowledge our shared fates, but in this new era, we are reimagining how funders can show up. At its heart, accompaniment is about a relationship of solidarity. Vini Bhansali, who leads the Solidaire Network, a community of donor organizers moving resources to justice movements, describes accompaniment "as a truly lateral relationship. It is a donor orientation that's about learning from our partners and being led by their strategies. Accompaniment allows us to invest in experimentation and imagination."[33] Accompaniment stands in stark contrast to Carnegie's belief that funders know best, instead recognizing that movements and funders have different, complimentary roles to play in advancing change.

7. Investing in People

The final area for philanthropy on this list cuts across specific issues and is quite simply investing in the people who are doing the most important work of our times. We take for granted that nonprofit work is done out of care and therefore tends to be poorly compensated. But that is a choice that has been made for too long by the philanthropic sector. Increased demand and workload as well as low wages have contributed to high rates of burnout in the nonprofit sector. Rusty Stahl, president and CEO of Fund the People, said, "Grantmakers are missing the fundamental connections between their own funding practices, how grantees can compensate staff, why burnout is on the upswing, and how all of this damages the ability of grantors and grantees alike to achieve their shared goals."[34]

In this new era of philanthropy, let's generously resource the work of building a more just and sustainable future so that organizations have sustainable staffing, good benefits, and time for rest and sabbaticals. Let's build robust leadership pipelines and cross-movement networks and infrastructure. Let's invest abundantly in the people who are doing the work of building a better future.

As we forge this next era, we must continue to evolve our understanding of the best fields for philanthropy and continue to cocreate this list with those who are leading the work to build a more just and sustainable future.

Then and Now: From Gilded Philanthropy to a New Era

		GILDED AGE PHILANTHROPY	NEW ERA OF PHILANTHROPY
	What is the story of this philanthropy?	This is a story about an individual's great generosity. It's a philanthropy that says, we can afford to live in inequitable systems that generate harm because philanthropy will tend to those harms.	This is a collective story about the transformation we can accomplish together. It's about who we can be when we reach across class and race in solidarity to build a better future for all of us.
	What is this philanthropy's relationship to structures of power?	Funding covers harms caused by unjust systems, while leaving in place who wields wealth and power.	Invests in systemic change and shifting power, transforming structures to prioritize people over profits.
	What is at the heart of this philanthropy?	The donor, the person or institution with wealth, is at the center of this philanthropy.	The aspirational freedom dreams of communities are the heart of this philanthropy.
	What does this philanthropy build?	Physical infrastructure like libraries, parks, concert halls, and hospital wings.	Responsive and relational infrastructures, including new frameworks, new narratives, and cross-organizational networks.
	Who has decision-making power in this philanthropy?	Donors and trustees, who often lack proximity to issues and communities, retain decision-making power with little public accountability.	The new era reimagines philanthropic governance to include expertise, proximity, and accountability.
	Who benefits from this philanthropy?	The donor reaps multiple financial and societal benefits as a result of their philanthropy.	The community benefits as resources are returned and people gain more voice and power in the decisions that impact their lives.
	What changes as a result of this philanthropy?	There are positive impacts, but fundamentally, very little changes.	Transformation becomes possible, of systems and ourselves too.

PRACTICE PROMPTS

Then and Now

Review the "Then and Now" table and consider where your actions or beliefs remain in the past. Are there places where you are trying to move from one era to the next? Identify the support you need to move into the next era.

Reflection Exercise

Journal about how you understand the purpose of philanthropy in these times.

Ask and Listen to Grantseekers

Learn directly from nonprofits about how they experience gilded philanthropy. For example, on social media, an email list, a grantee newsletter, or a survey as a version of this prompt:

Describe a time when you had an experience with a funder that expressed the worldview that "the wealthy know best."

Digest the responses and reflect on where in philanthropic practice these ideas are still thriving.

"Some Good" to "Most Good"

As a team, draw a spectrum of some good to most good, and map out your giving. Reflect on the map and discuss what it will take to move from some good to the most possible good.

Reimagine Governance

Any vision of a more just future includes governance that is democratic and rooted in care. The work of philanthropic governance today requires us to innovate and evolve the structures we operate within. It means building new muscles, envisioning new relationships, and infusing new meaning that is a better fit for these times. This chapter draws on interviews with trustees, foundation leaders, and philanthropy-serving organization staff. I explore what holds us back from more effective governance and share breakthroughs that boards can make to meet this moment.

It had been a big day for Julian Corner, Lankelly Chase Foundation's chief executive officer. After sixty years of existence, Lankelly Chase, the seventy-ninth largest foundation in Great Britain and a funder of social justice organizations, announced that they would be moving all their resources into community ownership.[1] In five years, they would cease to exist as an organization. I met Julian on the day of this announcement, and my first question to him was, "How did your board make this decision?" Julian laughed. "That's the question I've been asked dozens of times today."

The following morning Julian and I shared a plenary stage at the Next Frontiers in Funding, Philanthropy and Investment conference in London, where our task was to set up a day of conversations about philanthropy in times of crisis and opportunity to an audience of over a thousand attendees.

Julian and I had talked through different aspects of the announcement and what he would speak about on the panel. The foundation's decision to move their capital into community ownership itself was significant. Julian wanted to inspire other philanthropies to recognize the role they play in "upholding colonialism capitalism," in hopes that they would come to a similar conclusion. But in his conversations—with journalists, grantee partners, funders, and me—few people questioned the *decision* itself. What everyone wanted to know was, "How did your *board* come to this decision?"

Media coverage of Lankelly Chase's announcement reflected this interest in governance, with the *Guardian* reporting: "Lankelly Chase's trustee board had become increasingly unable to reconcile its charitable mission to tackle racism, injustice, and inequality with its position as a major investor in global capital markets it considers to be rooted in racial and colonial exploitation."[2]

That is where Julian decided to ground his remarks at the conference, reflecting on governance—how his board came to this decision. He noted, "The idea of dismantling Lankelly Chase is not particularly a surprise to people—that idea is in the field. What is surprising to people is that we were actually able to act on it. Which tells me that *governance is viewed somehow as a principal blocker to shift and move in this field.*"

Effective Philanthropic Governance for Our Times

Lankelly Chase's story is not the story of every foundation, but it brings to the center an important question: What constitutes effective governance in these times? And how must today's governance evolve?

Philanthropic governance is an issue that deserves more care, candor, and attention. Effective philanthropic governance transforms assets from being "my money" to being resources held in the public trust. Whether philanthropy will be able to transform itself to meet this moment of crisis and opportunity will depend in large part on whether we can evolve the governance of our institutions. At its best, governance upholds and reflects our deepest-held values. It is proximate, responsive, and a collective endeavor. At its worst, and too often in our sector, it is extractive, slow-moving, disconnected, and working with conflicted interests.

The Rules for Who Makes the Rules

What is governance? The purpose of nonprofit governance is to provide oversight and accountability and to support an organization in meeting its purpose. Of course, there is governance in theory, and in practice. There are the fundamental fiduciary duties of care, loyalty, and obedience as well as bylaws specific to each organization. And then there is the felt, lived experience of governance, how we understand the mix of ultimate responsibility, accountability, and decision-making authority, and how we experience the power that is held by trustees. I appreciate this description of governance offered by consultant Tracy Kunkler of Circle Forward Partners, an organization that supports nonprofits to design collaborative governance structures:

> Governance is how we set up systems to live our values and leads to the creation, reinforcement, or reproduction of social norms and institutions. Governance systems give form to the culture's power relationships. It becomes *the rules for who makes the rules and how.*[3]

Philanthropy as a sector is marked by a deep power imbalance, and in this context, foundation trustees hold a disproportionate amount of control. That philanthropic governance is viewed by many as a "principal blocker" of progress, and yet the topic of governance receives so little attention or scrutiny, is further proof of how much power is at play. The work of foundation trustees is both extremely consequential and largely opaque.

The good news is that trustees are positioned to be powerful forces for progress. A challenge is that they are rarely seen as such and rarely see themselves in this way. Too often, brilliant staff working in philanthropy spend their time trying to change everything else, avoiding one of the most impactful arenas for change: governance. In the philanthropic sector, governance is too often conflated with attending board meetings. When I was a new foundation executive director, I recall an experienced foundation leader counseling me to view board meetings as "performance art" and to design them accordingly. In other words, create "an experience" of governance, but not the conditions for truly practicing it.

Our low expectations for philanthropic governance reflect the moment we live in and a broader crisis in governance across sectors. We live in times of rising authoritarianism and unchecked corporate power. Whether we are talking about airplane manufacturers giving short shrift to safety,[4] or rewriting school curriculums to say that enslaved people benefited from slavery,[5] the real story behind the headlines is a failure of governance.

Lankelly Chase's story underscores something essential that funders rarely acknowledge: How we govern, who gets to govern, and how trustees view their role as stewards is not set in stone. In "The Four Principles of Purpose-Driven Board Leadership," Anne Wallestad, former president and CEO of Board-Source, notes that "this is both the beauty and the challenge of a board structure: Only a board has the power to change itself, and boards can interpret and apply their own expectations of their roles and responsibilities. In most of the ways that matter, boards are their own accountability mechanism."[6]

Public Governance for a Public Purpose: A Surprising History Lesson on Foundation Governance

Philanthropic governance models have traditionally centered the power of donors and have provided little opportunity for public scrutiny and accountability. The dominant approach we see today is characterized by three key traits: low transparency, low accountability, and low proximity. A brief history lesson helps us understand the origins of the private philanthropy governance model we have today and highlights that it was not inevitable.

With his massive earnings from Standard Oil, John D. Rockefeller was one of the wealthiest Americans ever to live. While his philanthropy is widely recognized, the story of how he tried, and initially failed, to get his foundation started is less known.

Rob Reich recalls this history in his book *Just Giving: Why Philanthropy Is Failing Democracy and How It Can Do Better*, and the following facts and details are drawn from his book. Rockefeller wanted to create a $100 million (over $2 billion in today's dollars) general-purpose foundation to tackle widespread social issues. At the time, no foundation of this proposed size and scale existed. Between 1909 and 1913, Rockefeller and his advisers worked to obtain a federal charter to create the foundation. His plans were met with fierce opposition and widespread apprehension, including concerns about governance, public accountability, and lack of transparency. As Reich describes, "Louis Brandeis, the future Supreme Court justice, said that the Rockefeller Foundation was 'inconsistent with our democratic aspirations' and confessed to 'grave apprehensions' about the power that was lodged in the hands of a few wealthy men."[7]

To allay these concerns, Rockefeller made a series of concessions, including a proposal that the governance of the foundation be partially public, making the work of the foundation formally accountable to the broader community. Rockefeller's proposal made the board of trustees subject to a veto by a majority of a congressionally appointed board consisting of various political leaders, including the President of the United States, the President of the Senate, the Speaker of the House, the chief justice of the US Supreme Court, and education leaders that included the presidents of Harvard, Yale, Columbia, Johns Hopkins, and the University of Chicago. Other concessions that Rockefeller made included limiting the foundation's lifespan to fifty years, with an option to extend to one hundred years pending approval by Congress, and capping the size of the foundation at $100 million, with a requirement to spend all income earned from the endowment annually. If this had passed, the Rockefeller Foundation would have spent down and shut its doors by 2013, one hundred years after its founding.

These concessions, while dramatic from today's perspective, were not enough to allay concerns. After almost four years of effort, in 1913, the charter failed to pass the Senate. Rockefeller swiftly brought it to the New

York state legislature, where it was approved—without a single concession that Rockefeller had offered at the federal level. Reich notes, "Had the US Senate passed the House bill to approve the Rockefeller Foundation, it would have created a legal template for the institutional design of foundations with limits on size and time and provisions for clear public oversight."[8]

What does this little-known story tell us a century later, in these still unequal times, when our democratic institutions are under attack? First, it is striking how the public responses to early foundations were critical and cautious, whereas today foundations are largely met with gratitude and greenlighting. Importantly, the clear call to balance the goals of philanthropy with the values of democracy through mechanisms for public accountability has gone unmet for more than a hundred years. To me, this history is a reminder that foundation governance could have been designed differently to promote accountability—and that it still can be structured differently today.

It is powerful to hear these voices from the not-so-distant past reminding us: It can be another way. Today, we too can say, from a place not of concessions but of proclamation: Work that has a public purpose needs public accountability.

Philanthropic Governance Barriers and Breakthroughs

Transformative philanthropy is impossible in the absence of effective governance. This belief was shared by almost every philanthropic leader I interviewed for this book. Thankfully, many of them and their peers are working to build the conditions for change. In this section, I describe three often identified barriers to effective philanthropic governance and stories of people and organizations that are reimagining governance to break through these barriers.

A Governance Time Crunch: Bridging the Gap Between Capacity and Commitment

When it comes to time, there is a profound gap between capacity and need. A 2015 Center for Effective Philanthropy report, *Benchmarking Foundation Governance,* found that the median number of times that foundation boards meet annually is four, with each board meeting lasting around four hours.[9] Of course, trustees will note that they work between meetings, so let's assume that foundation trustees are meeting, on average, for sixteen hours annually, and overall are contributing thirty-two hours of labor and leadership annually. A foundation executive director described this "impossible situation," saying about her board, "I come to them with big things like our theory of change, and they are zooming in from a different reality of their jobs and life. They're expected and having to make decisions on these huge things that they don't work on day to day."

Nick Tedesco, president and CEO of the National Center for Family Philanthropy, sums up this challenge of modern philanthropic governance by noting that boards are "part-time decision-makers for full-time decisions." Nick has a point. Trustees are charged with making so many decisions, from strategy to investments to spending. With the limited time that they have, it's no wonder trustees and staff who work with them experience this reality as impossible. And in these turbulent and volatile times, where conditions rapidly change, the impact of having part-time decision-makers is that foundations struggle to be responsive and nimble, instead taking years to make needed pivots.

The breakthrough that boards can make is a delegation of decision-making authority to those who have both the time and relevant expertise required to make informed decisions. Today more boards are delegating grantmaking approval to staff or participatory committees composed of community members. The Surdna Foundation had a governance structure in place since the 1990s in which board members reviewed and approved hundreds of grants each year through three Board program committees.[10] Reviewing these grants was time-intensive, and the structure of the committees reinforced a siloed view of the foundation's work. When an internal board self-assessment "urged a shift of board members' attention from grant approvals to deeper learning rooted in outcomes and social impact," the board voted to phase out the grant approval committees and moved toward an "ambitious new learning and impact agenda."[11] Delegation of grantmaking decisions often brings in more expertise while leaving boards with more time to spend on bigger strategic questions and decisions.

Of course, delegating decisions only really works if there is a culture of trust. Regan Pritzker, a trustee of the Libra Foundation, describes Libra's board as working within "a chain of trust," where the board trusts and delegates to the president, who in turn trusts and delegates to the staff, who can then operate with trust with the communities that they are resourcing. In Regan's description of this process, I hear how interdependent trust and delegation are, and how critical the board's role is to build a culture of trust within an organization. In this new era of philanthropy, a key governance function for trustees is to build this chain and culture of trust, understanding that the ultimate beneficiaries are grantees and the communities they serve.

The Crucial Question of Who Governs and How We Shift Power

Lankelly Chase's decision to move their assets into community control began two and a half years before Julian Corner walked onto the plenary stage, when the foundation overhauled its governance and sought out new trustees from the community. Julian describes approaching potential board members in the community, asking, "Please come to our organization and help us change." Their question back to him was, "But are you prepared to change?" The recruited community leaders wanted to be engaged—but only as equal decision-makers. They wanted real power, not to serve as symbolic community representatives on the margins of a board.

Julian noted that when he agreed, he didn't fully realize what he was saying yes to, but he knew he had to give up on "a whole load of certainties that have taken me to this point of being a CEO of a foundation." He could not have guessed that this governance overhaul, deepened by the board's new members, would lead a few short years later to the board's decision to transfer all the foundation's resources and power back to communities and close the institution's doors.

Foundations are institutions incorporated with a public purpose. Yet, there is an unspoken and often unchallenged norm in the sector: Those with resources, or those connected to resources, are the ones who fulfill this most important role of governance, resulting in a mismatch between the public purpose of the foundation and those charged with overseeing the realization of it.

Many trustees are tasked with powerful governance roles because of their proximity to the original donor rather than proximity to the issues, a needed skill set, or a commitment to the foundation's mission. For example, in family philanthropy, foundation boards are often composed of trustees who represent multiple generations of the family of the original donor. While some foundations screen family trustees for expertise and support of the mission, other criteria unrelated to the mission, like "branch of the family," also make it into trustee eligibility criteria.

Wealth is racialized, and therefore building governance structures based on proximity to wealth contributes to a profound racial gap in governance. In 2017, Board Source's *Leading with Intent* survey of foundation boards found that 40 percent of boards surveyed had board leadership that was all white.[12] In their survey of 111 foundations, only 15 percent of board members were people of color. There is an important role for people with resources or specific skill sets to play in accompanying those who are more proximate to the work. And proximity to the communities who are intended to benefit from the resources of a foundation brings immeasurable benefit to the project of governance and to the work of giving overall.

Today, many boards are realizing that too many lived experiences and perspectives are missing from foundation boards, to the detriment of the board's overall effectiveness. As family foundations that have long been governed by family members and descendants begin to open their boards to community representatives, there must be an explicit equity among the board members. It is not unusual for family foundations to create different types of board memberships, creating a limit of terms for nonfamily board members, and unlimited terms for family board members. This perpetuates a sense that some people are at the table in a symbolic role, while others are real board members.

An example of a power-shifting breakthrough in governance comes from the Kolibri Foundation, a family foundation set up to resource BIPOC-led social movements. When Eileen, Steve, and Leo Farbman were creating the Kolibri Foundation, they knew they wanted to do it in a way that "does not reinforce the cultural and systemic pain" associated with traditional philanthropic practice.[13] They built this commitment into their governance structure by designing their board so that the majority of trustees are social movement leaders, not family members. Further, they structured their bylaws so that nonfamily board members would always be the majority of the board and would even have the ability to vote out family members if they wished.

Identity and the Psychology of Wealth as Barriers: Moving from Privilege to Progress

When I asked Eileen Farbman, a cofounder and trustee of Kolibri Foundation, about the decision that her family made to give majority control of the board to movement leaders, she shared that her peers told her they "would never do this because their identity is wrapped around being a philanthropist." Eileen had worked as a philanthropist for thirty years when she and her family set up Kolibri. She describes making an "intentional decision to cede control, to say, I can take off the philanthropy hat and lean into this trust." Eileen also described how glad she was to have made this decision, and shared all the ways that the foundation's grantmaking benefits from the expertise of movement leaders who serve on the board.

The role of identity was a recurring theme in my interviews about philanthropic governance. I heard about the deep personalization that some trustees bring to the work. Sometimes this manifests as a strong desire to do the work and do it well. A CEO friend shared that a board member once told her, "I don't want to just be a resource as a checkbook. I want to be a human resource, a value-added resource, a capacity resource." I also heard numerous stories about how trustees' desires for connection and meaning were impacting the foundation's ability to do its work. For example, when a billion-dollar foundation, where the board still approves every single grant, was advised to change this process, a board member said, "I know we need to stop, but I can't. If I don't approve grants, what am I doing?" Across numerous interviews, there was a thread about the negative impact of trustees operating with excess personalization, where the conflation of their roles as trustees with their individual identities leads to controlling behaviors and decision-making that doesn't further the mission.

I also heard about an emotional attachment that some trustees feel to the foundation's resources, such that they approach foundation spending as if it were the same as spending their own money. This challenge is captured in stories about foundation boards celebrating when an institution's assets increase due to market gains, rather than celebrating grantee partner wins and accomplishments. Where funds are in an endowment or a donor-advised fund, an overidentification with the resources, and the habits that go with a "my money" story, rarely serve the governance needs of the organization.

Identity in and of itself doesn't have to be a barrier. Nor is it fixed. There are numerous identities that offer breakthroughs for trustees to channel their commitment to the work in ways that enhance governance. The key is that trustees must bring to their work awareness of their power and privilege and clarity about the foundation's purpose—that it is there to affirm and serve the community rather than the trustees. Rachel Humphrey, senior director of Practice Acceleration at Justice Funders, works with foundation boards that are seeking to adopt liberatory governance approaches. She begins her work with trustees by asking them to recall an experience in which someone in their lives held power positively. This inquiry helps trustees recognize the power in their roles and work toward ways of using that power for the greater good.

Before I share identities that can enhance governance, I want to share a cautionary note. Identities are not fixed, and in turbulent times people sometimes revert to their default identities. For this reason, it is important that in times of crisis, trustees bring even greater awareness to how identity is shaping their governance approach and are clear about their values and how they show up in their roles.

Here are six identities that trustees can embody that will lead toward more transformational governance:

Partner: This is the simplest identity, and yet it is a meaningful shift from how some trustees embody their role. Instead of governing from hierarchy and power, this identity offers a pathway based on shared values and responsibilities. At its best, the work of governance is deeply relational. Most CEOs are seeking a partnership with their board and want a board that will walk side by side with them through these challenging times. An organization in which the board serves as a partner to the CEO is much better positioned to meet this moment and to be responsive. Trustees can see their role as being a partner to those who have expertise, as well as to the communities served by the foundation.

In solidarity: Solidarity requires that trustees understand the history of their wealth accumulation and are committed to shifting power in their philanthropic relationships.[14] Leah Hunt-Hendrix and Astra Taylor, coauthors of *Solidarity: The Past, Present, and Future of a World-Changing Idea,* share, "When funders are guided by the principles of transformative solidarity and see themselves as partners with working-class and poor movements, rather than as their patrons, they are better positioned to align their resources behind efforts to create more just systems of wealth accumulation and distribution."[15] An identity of solidarity supports cross-class and cross-racial relationships and affirms mutuality. Trustee leadership rooted in this truth of interdependence leads to a transformational resourcing of a more just future.

Movers of wealth: Nick Tedesco, president and CEO of the National Center for Family Philanthropy, describes how trustees can shift from seeing themselves as "holders of wealth" to being "movers of wealth." This shift reminds us that trustees are doing their job when they are moving and returning capital to communities. Farhad Ebrahimi, founder of the Chorus Foundation, which sunsetted in 2024, reflected on the possibilities that come with a new role as,

> a liberating process.... We're actually deeply asking people to show up as protagonists and agents, just in a way that's very different from what they've been encouraged to do.... It's about saying, there are ways in which people deeply need you to show up, and leadership.... But it's not about deciding where money goes in other people's communities.[16]

The "Should we do more?" board: When I first became executive director of the General Service Foundation, I was lovingly coached by peers to be careful about the timing or size of my requests to the board. So many of us have learned to tread with caution in what we ask of board members. And yet, when I went to the executive committee twice during my first year in the job with big asks, they said yes both times. In particular, one board member consistently added, "Should we do more?" And so, I came to call them (lovingly) the "Should we do more?" board.

In a sector that is so risk-averse, "Should we do more?" is not just a question but an organizational stance that shapes how the board sees their role. Often, we think of governance as the responsibility to limit and avoid risk. But the truth is, change is not possible without risk. Governance for these times involves rethinking our relationship to risk and learning to take the needed risks wisely and together when our values and purpose are at stake. Put another way, governance in this new era requires trustees to have courage and take risks.

A reimagined twenty-first century steward: To be a steward in these times isn't simply to maintain resources in their current form, but rather to facilitate the transfer of these resources to communities, to facilitate the alchemy that will transform resources into a more just future.

Stewardship is the "careful and responsible management of something entrusted to one's care."[17] This idea of stewardship of resources has roots in numerous other contexts, like trusts, in which trustees are literally charged with managing an asset. Stewardship is often understood as growing and maintaining the asset so that it can be there for future beneficiaries.

Yet philanthropic institutions are more than an asset or a pot of money to be managed or grown. Foundations are mission-based organizations with a central purpose, and they are charged with the public trust. A trustee's responsibility of stewardship is a responsibility to realize the mission and serve the public trust. Stewardship of a mission requires not just growing resources but spending them to advance the mission.

On a recent walk in Muir Woods in Northern California, I heard a park ranger describe stewardship as "the idea of what we want to pass on." This idea reminds us that stewardship is also about the *impact* of our spending, and how our giving will shape the world we are passing on.

A mission-driven fiduciary: The fiduciary duties of trustees are ripe for reimagining. To be a fiduciary is to act in the best interests of the beneficiary and not from a place of your own interests. Foundation trustees have fiduciary duties of care, loyalty, and obedience, and each of these are opportunities for trustees to govern for the future that the foundation's mission envisions.

The Heron Foundation's investment policy statement is a great example of how fiduciary duties and stewardship are being reimagined:

> We believe that the fiduciary responsibilities of all philanthropic institutions mean that we have *both a duty of obedience to our specific mission and a duty of obedience to a larger public purpose.*... Heron believes that our *fiduciary duties of care require that our actions not detract from the long-term interest of those whom we intend to benefit* by our philanthropy.[18]

Care, loyalty, a larger public purpose. How might we see more progress if foundation boards center care and their broader public purpose in their decision-making? What becomes more possible when trustees lean into our role as stewards of a more just and sustainable future for all? How might a deeper governance emerge when trustees see themselves as stewards of the more just future that will be passed on as a result of a foundation's work?

The Tempting Appeal of No Governance as the Best Governance

It is essential that we remember this: The creation of governance structures quite literally takes the resources and work of the foundation out of the control of the founding donors and puts it into a more collective structure that is intended to be accountable. Frustration with philanthropic governance as a barrier to progress runs high these days. And so, it should not surprise us that one growing trend in the sector is the bypassing of governance and transparency altogether through the use of LLCs, donor-advised funds (DAFs), and other directed giving approaches.

Donor-advised funds have been growing in popularity, with the number of donor-advised accounts nearly doubled since 2008, growing to almost two million in 2023.[19] Why has there been this rise in giving through DAFs? The media focus on DAFs centers on how they offer a highly sought-after tax benefit—they allow donors to take a full tax deduction for money deposited into a DAF, even before the money has been granted out to nonprofits. Further, once the money is put into a DAF, it can grow tax-free. While these tax-related perks are often cited to explain the increase in DAFS, I suspect the increase also has to do with a perception that DAFs allow donors to move funds without the "red tape" of traditional foundation governance. Providers of DAFs promote quick and easy grantmaking—something that is challenging for some private foundations. Donors are also drawn to the anonymity that they can have with DAFs, which allows them to avoid public scrutiny of their giving. DAFs require even less transparency than private foundations, and the rise in DAFs suggests that the philanthropic sector is moving toward even greater opacity.

Beyond DAFs, many of the largest donors today have structured their giving in a way that diminishes or sidesteps governance altogether. Some of today's most visible large donors have indicated a reluctance to cede this control. One of the largest foundations in the world, the Gates Foundation, was governed for more than a decade by a board of the two founding donors, Bill and Melinda Gates, along with Bill Gates Sr. and their close friend Warren Buffet. In 2021, when Bill and Melinda Gates announced their divorce, they began the process of building a governance structure for the foundation, announcing in a press release, "The cochairs have also decided to expand the number of trustees overseeing the foundation's governance and decision-making as a family charitable trust. The additional trustees will bring new perspectives, help guide resource allocation and strategic direction, and ensure the stability and sustainability of the foundation."[20] While adding independent trustees is an important step forward, the *New York Times* reported that the newly formed board does not have control over the endowment, which is held in a separate trust.[21] MacKenzie Scott, a large donor who has received praise for conducting her giving in ways that are less burdensome on the field as well as her support of grassroots organizations, conducts her giving through the Bridgespan Group, sidestepping a visible, and therefore accountable, governance mechanism.

Is Our Governance Reflective of the Past, or the More Just Future We Seek to Build?

We have forgotten the inherent worth and potential of governance, and how it can be an embodiment of care for the broader public purpose. Through governance, we get to practice hard things like coming together for the greater good. I believe that in these consequential times, philanthropic governance is a site of possibility.

When I think of all the boards I've spoken to, worked with, and served on, it is clear to me that there's no template for what an ideal governance structure is, nor a single answer for what success looks like. To some, it means engaging more deeply with grantee partners. For others, it means deepening their political education and commitment to supporting community change. For many boards, it involves revisiting the places where gilded philanthropy's blueprint lives in the governance design.

In this new era, boards are approaching these questions with rigorous inquiry—revisiting decisions made in bygone eras that impact how the foundation shows up today. The Lankelly Chase board decided to move its resources to community control; that won't be the right move for all foundations, but their willingness to ask difficult questions and examine their place within the broader ecosystem is a model for how brave and strategic governance can lead to real transformation. It is a clear example of the kind of governance that these times call for. Lankelly Chase's Julian Corner shared:

> If you want people to meaningfully hold power in a governance role, they have to step into becoming the organization, seeing themselves as responsible for and in part complicit in the legacy structures of that organization. They must start to hold accountability for its efficient running even while they believe it should fundamentally change, take flack for the old system that they didn't create even while yearning for the new.

Julian notes a trustee describing philanthropic governance as "needing to be the thing while trying to change the thing."[22]

We can start by connecting the dots between the democracy we practice in our institutions and the true democracy many of us are working toward in our grantmaking. We can replace old mental models, like "People with the most money have the most power," with a commitment to more inclusive practices that are informed by people with deep expertise in the challenges and opportunities that communities face. We can keep coming back to the purpose of our organizations. As we bring these new muscles as well as creativity and care into philanthropic governance, we will dramatically shift our institution's ability to meet the challenges of these times.

PRACTICE PROMPT

Trustee Fishbowl on Reimagining Governance

Step 1. Invite your board of directors to read this chapter.

Step 2. Set up chairs in a circle and have two to four chairs in an inner circle.

Step 3. Invite two to four board members into the circle, and use one or more of the prompts below to start the fishbowl conversation.

1. What does twenty-first-century stewardship require of us?

2. How does our governance model reflect the world we wish to see and build?

3. How might we embed greater public accountability and transparency in our governance approach?

4. What most scares you about ceding control as a trustee and leaning into trust?

5. Which reimagined trustee identities will further our work in these times the most?

Step 4. Participants in the outside circle can enter the fishbowl at any time, by tapping the shoulder of someone in the inner circle. The conversation can evolve, using these prompts as a starting point.

Step 5. Capture ideas and possibilities for strengthening governance and delegate these to a governance committee.

Bend Time

Assumptions about how to be with and in time permeate our philanthropic practice. Yet too often our approach is out of step with what is needed and at stake now. This chapter offers eleven invitations to reimagine our relationship to time, so that we may meet the challenges of this consequential moment.

1. The Clock of the World

The activist and philosopher Grace Lee Boggs famously asked, "What time is it on the clock of the world?" This new era of philanthropy requires us to ask this question so that we may unlearn and relearn our relationship to time. Rather than seeing time as a fixed number of interchangeable days, we must develop a heightened awareness of the specificity of this moment and what it requires.

In philanthropy, how we think about time is informed by habit and internal organizational demands. For example, your grantmaking may be organized into spring and fall cycles, timed to match a schedule of board meetings. Yet not every spring or fall is similar; nor do needs fall in cycle with board meetings. Rather, every time comes with its own needs and opportunities.

In 2019, at General Service Foundation, which I led for seven years, our team adopted a "2021 mind-set." While none of us foresaw the global pandemic of 2020, we could look ahead and anticipate that 2020 would be a consequential year. Nonprofits working to protect our democracy have long complained that funding comes in too late. We wanted our grantee partners to go into 2020, and beyond, having the resources they needed to staff appropriately and spend their time on the most important work—not on applying for grants. We shifted our budget and grants cycles to make our 2020 grants early.

I was reminded of this when I saw the Democracy Fund's "All by April" open letter in 2024, signed by 170 pro-democracy donors and foundations who pledged to make early grant commitments and grants to nonprofits in the 2024 election year so that organizations could recruit talent and build out the capacities they needed.[1] Together the "All by April" funders pledged $140 million in early funding, understanding that there are windows of opportunity in which grantmaking can have an outsize impact.

When funders treat all time as the same, we risk overlooking perhaps the most important quality of time: the fact that what we do today directly impacts what will be needed, or even possible, tomorrow.

2. Forever Time

In perpetuity is defined as "for all time; forever."[2] Many private foundations operate with a goal of existing in perpetuity. This idea of foreverness itself feels like it's from another time. Our contemporary sensibilities skew more toward impermanence. Today, we know that so many things we thought would be around forever—glaciers, many species, the Gulf Stream system—will likely not be. Yet perpetuity as an operating principle powerfully shapes today's philanthropy. Every day, trustees make decisions that put the goal of foundation foreverness first, and the urgent needs that exist today second.

Prioritizing foreverness requires a certain downplaying of the present and near-future times. Forever is about the *very far* future. Perpetuity is such a powerful norm in the sector that many foundations operate in service of it, even when it is not an explicit mandate set out in their bylaws or charters. Many trustees of perpetual foundations will tell you that *they* did not make the decision about foreverness. They are just the stewards of a decision that was already made. And yet, each time trustees approve a spending decision or a budget that is aimed at protecting the foundation's ability to exist forever, they are perpetuating the idea that forever time for the foundation is more important than this time and those who are living in it.

There have been objections to perpetuity for as long as there have been foundations. These objections include concerns about how perpetuity removes accountability, dilutes impact, and fuels generational inequality. In *Just Giving,* Rob Reich summarizes nineteenth-century philosopher John Stuart Mill's views on perpetuity: "'Under the guise of fulfilling a bequest' a foundation transforms a 'dead man's intentions for a single day' into a 'rule for subsequent centuries.'"[3] Early writings on perpetuity have this vivid and macabre quality to them, with cautionary verses warning against the power of the "dead hand."

Could perpetuity be a strategic approach to impact? It is possible, in some specific cases, but overall the philanthropic sector's track record suggests that the forever goal creates a structural approach to funding that is slow and stingy, with most private foundations giving close to the legally required minimum of 5 percent each year, regardless of the needs and opportunities.[4] A perpetuity goal differs from other goals because to achieve it, you must prioritize the foundation's existence over the actual thing that the foundation is supposed to achieve. To put it plainly, if your charitable mission requires more investment today, you may find your perpetuity goal to be in conflict with your mission.

I don't usually think of English common law as my go-to place for wisdom. And still, I am reminded of a dreaded bar exam topic: the Rule Against Perpetuities, a property law, not applicable to charities, that limited the extent to which people living today can impose restrictions on property in the very far future. The rule reflected a concern that English judges had about the dead being able to impose excessive limitations on the ownership and use of property by those still living. The prescience of these concerns does have me wondering whether we may need a new Rule Against Perpetuity to require foundation trustees to prioritize the needs *in these times* over the forever times.

3. Market Time

True or false: When stock market returns are down, foundation spending will go down too. I wish this statement were false, and instead, grantee needs and social change opportunities were the barometer for philanthropic spending. After all, stock market declines often reflect anticipated pain points in the economy, like a recession or inflation, that are felt most intensely in communities with fewer resources. It would be logical for foundations to spend more, not less, in economically challenging times. But as of now, this statement is true. The state of the stock market, not grantee needs or social change opportunities, is a reliable predictor of foundation spending.[5]

So how do foundations make the pivotal and consequential decision of how much to spend each year? After all, spending is philanthropy's core tool to achieve its mission. Most foundations have something called a "spending policy" that describes the process by which the spending amount gets calculated. I use the word *calculated* intentionally. At most foundations, the process involves entering numbers into a calculator: the endowment size multiplied by a percentage, which equals the amount that a foundation will spend. The percentages entered into the calculator usually hover around 5 percent, the Internal Revenue Service's minimum required distribution for private foundations.

Traditional spending policy:

endowment value × ___% = foundation spending amount

In the traditional spending-policy formula, every year is an interchangeable unit. The specificities of a particular time, and what can be accomplished in it, do not find their way into this important decision of how much a foundation will spend.

In 2020 I published an article titled "A 'Balancing Test' for Foundation Spending" in the *Stanford Social Innovation Review* that offers a reimagined spending policy. I explain in the article that spending policies "are the invisible architecture shaping a variety of critical decisions about how a foundation will further its mission. To put it simply, if budget decisions are about how to slice the pie of available funds, spending policies determine how big the pie itself will be."[6]

The article's timing made it particularly resonant. In response to the pandemic and growing movements for racial justice, many foundations were taking a fresh look at their spending policies. Foundation leaders were hungry for a new approach and many funders went on to use the article to move beyond a market-time approach to spending.

This new spending policy approach resonated because funders agreed that good spending decisions must grapple with more than numbers. An effective spending policy must ask, *What is required of us in the world, right now?* How can we meet this moment? The key to a spending policy is that it is grounded in time. A calculator cannot account for the living, breathing change happening at this moment.

The article describes a spending policy approach that has decision-makers balance seven factors to determine their spending amount. Below is a summary of these factors and associated questions. Even if these questions are asked by the same group in the same organization, the answers will change over time because what's happening with the world, and with our grantee partners, keeps evolving.

Investment Returns

What is our investment philosophy, and how are we using our investments to further our mission?

Growth Goals

What is our institution's growth goal, how does the goal relate to our mission, and what can we do once we've met it?

Balancing Test for Foundation Spending

Perpetuity

How do we understand perpetuity? What is its purpose in these times, and how does it relate to our mission? Who is served by our perpetuity goal?

Meeting the Moment

What is at stake in this moment?

Organizational Values and Mission

What is the opportunity in this moment to live into our values and fulfill our mission?

Grants and Programs

In the coming year, what does our grantee community need? What opportunities and risks are they facing?

Administrative Costs

How do our administrative costs align with our organizational values?

4. Move Beyond Tiny Chunks of Time

Grants often come with a term, a period in which the money is spent. While a small number of funders are moving toward five- to ten-year-long grants (amazing! necessary!), on average grant terms are one or two years. The imposition of tiny timelines for change incentivizes grantseekers to focus on small things that can be changed rapidly and measured easily, rather than take on the big fundamental transformations that take time.

I was a funder for many years before I heard of a five-year grant. It was late 2015, and I had recently joined the Solidaire donor network.[7] A call went out on the email list asking donors to invest in Black-led movement-building organizations by making five-year grant commitments. Five years? I reflected on what a difference a five-year commitment from a donor would have made across my previous grant-supported work, what a runway it would have created. The donors in Solidaire met this request for long-term funding as if it were the most normal thing in the world. Witnessing individual donors make these five-year funding commitments inspired me to look at the grants we were making at General Service Foundation. I realized there was little reason that we couldn't make these longer commitments. After all, we had the funds in the bank.

One- and two-year grants may be the norm, and yet meaningful social change rarely occurs in small windows of time. Social change unfolds over a decade or two, a generation, half a century, or even longer.

Mia Birdsong, author of *How We Show Up* and *Freedom Revival,* writes about what it takes to build a collective future that serves us all.[8] Reflecting on the typical grant application question, "Please tell us how you will measure the impact of your work over the next two years," Mia notes, "I do my work knowing that it will come to fruition long after I am dead. The timeline that I am working with is a hundred years, so I don't know how to meaningfully answer that question. It is not how my work is set up."[9]

Jamie Allison, president of the Walter & Elise Haas Fund, saw that small time periods were limiting possibilities for grantees doing critical work. "Nonprofits need to have room to experiment," Jamie shared. "They need to have room to try new ideas. They also need stability—if an organization is getting small grants in one-year increments, it's hard to truly invest in staff and create stable high-quality programs and jobs."[10]

In conversations with community members, Jamie and her team learned that organizational and community change cycles happen over seven years. In 2023, they created the Endeavor Fund, which shifted grant terms from one year to seven years. This expansion was rooted in a belief that more time would fundamentally change not just the work itself but how it was practiced. Jamie shared, "We asked, If we commit to our grantee partners' visions, their mission, what would that look like? That would look like larger grants and supporting our partners like we want them to win, with room for experimentation, and investment in their organizations."[11]

5. Can We *Take* Less Time?

A few weeks after the 2016 election, as the magnitude of what a Trump presidency would mean for our grantees on the front lines of justice work was sinking in, I sat down to sign grant letters. I picked one up and read it closely for the first time. It was long and formal in tone, with standard philanthropic language setting out terms, conditions, and consequences if the conditions were not met.

> Grantee will submit a written narrative interim report, and a final report at the end of the grant. Failure to submit an interim report can result in withholding of second payment on grant.

We had just wrapped up a board meeting, where staff and board were united in our desire to stand with our grantees and for our values in this time of crisis. And yet, here were our letters, going out with checks, and so many conditions. I took my pen and began editing the much too long and far too punitive grant contract.

I crossed out the requirements of the interim and final written reports and replaced them with a forty-minute phone call with program officers. I knew from my own recent experience of being a grantee that a well-done report takes on average fourteen hours of staff time per donor—hurried responses might jeopardize future funding.

My goal that day was to liberate grantees from this burden that *we* had imposed on their time. When I asked our program staff how they used the written reports, they said it was for their learning. Phone calls made sense: forty minutes instead of fourteen hours, with the same goal and outcome of learning and the added benefit of deepening relationships. Imagine the cumulative time nonprofits would gain to devote to their core work if they were liberated from these outdated and burdensome reporting requirements from each and every one of their funders.

A few months later I received a postcard from the director of a grantee that worked with low-income immigrant communities in rural Colorado. The inscription was short and to the point: "Thank you for making it easier on reporting. This is a lot of stress every time." I kept that postcard on my desk for the next six years, as a reminder to pay attention to the impact of how we practice our philanthropy and the stress we cause by taking the precious resource of time from our grantees and their communities.

6. Spend the Time

How do funders spend their time? There are meetings and memos and paperwork, but the most meaningful and least explicitly valued part of working in philanthropy is the relationships we have an opportunity to build, and those require a meaningful investment of time. When we set up our philanthropic infrastructures to be in service of process and paperwork, staff working at the foundation rarely have the time necessary to build authentic relationships and partnerships.

While we like to think that money is our currency for change, in my experience it is actually our relationships that shape how impactful our grants will be. Relationships give context and meaning to the grant. If they are strong, healthy, and equitable, relationships give grantees the space to take risks, experiment, fail, and learn from failure. Relationships allow grantees to be honest about challenges and truthful about what it will really take to meet opportunities. Relationships with fellow funders are also important as these relationships help us work as part of a broader ecosystem. Relationships require nurture, and our organizations must be structured for an abundant spending of this kind of time.

7. Fund Not Only What Is Possible Now, but Also What May Become Possible in Another Time

When we resource work based solely on a sense of possibility in a particular moment, we lose the opportunity to lay the groundwork for possibilities that may develop. When things change, what is possible at a particular time can shift quickly. When grantees have core, flexible, general operating support, they can be responsive to what is possible at a given time, and pivot when there are changes.

Many of us were first introduced to the term *essential workers* when the pandemic hit and the lockdowns began. Essential workers included educators, caregivers, farmworkers, retail workers, tradespeople, transportation workers, and more. We saw them risk their lives doing the work that made it possible for office workers to stay home and stay safe. The truth is that these workers have always been essential—their contributions just weren't recognized.

Prior to the pandemic, there was a growing constellation of organizations working to develop a narrative strategy to uplift the dignity of low-wage workers who have long labored without basic rights. These organizations used this once-in-a-generation opening to reshape the narrative about these workers, to affirm them as essential and worthy of dignity, fair wages, and protections. What made it possible for organizations like Resilience Force, Caring Across Generations, National Domestic Workers Alliance, National Immigration Law Center, and others to step up when the times changed? The answer is grants that were flexible and long-term and not overly focused on the constraints of the times in which the grants were made.

Long-term flexible support is how we resource what may become possible—and essential—in another time.

8. Legacy as a Thread Connecting Past, Present, and Future Time

For some funders, legacy is an ever-present priority and concern. But when we talk about legacy, the subject is often the way that our present will be understood in the future. How will we be remembered? We might speak of legacies as stories about the generosity of great individuals or generous institutions.

Rarely do we engage with the most horrific parts of our country's past, or even the dark corners of the foundation's original wealth. Or the rich history of community resistance and resilience. Without this context, what can our legacies tell us? And how can we make sense of this time, where trillions of dollars sit in endowments, locked away and growing, rather than being spent to empower and uplift communities?

How we understand the past determines how we make sense of the present and the ways we can imagine the future. This is our moment to ask the unasked questions, to help us make sense of the present, so that we may imagine a new future.

9. Accelerate the Timeline for Justice

In 2001, my mentor Hope Lewis, a human rights scholar and law professor at Northeastern University School of Law, introduced me to Randall Robinson's book, *The Debt,* in which the author makes a passionate case for reparations.[12] In 2019, I shared with my board of directors David Brooks's opinion piece "The Case for Reparations," aptly subtitled "A Slow Convert to the Cause."[13] Brooks describes our country at a "moment of make-or-break racial reckoning." In the piece, Brooks notes that he read Ta-Nehisi Coates's 2014 *Atlantic* article "The Case for Reparations" nearly five years ago, with "mild disagreement."[14] Yet, his time traveling the country and studying America's history and divides moved him to conclude that reconciliation and repair and reparations are the way forward after all, as Coates's article made clear.

Four hundred years after the arrival of the first enslaved Africans in what was still the British colony of Virginia, journalist Nikole Hannah-Jones marked the anniversary with the groundbreaking 1619 Project to reexamine the legacy of slavery in America.[15] Four hundred years, eighteen years, five years. I am struck by how long it takes for good ideas to travel into the mainstream, and how long legacies of injustice persist. What can we do to accelerate the timelines for ideas whose time has come?

10. The Patience of a Thousand Years; the Urgency of Now

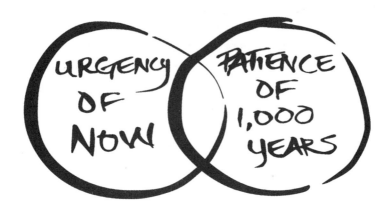

Can we go all-in on justice in a way that is timeless?

11. Time Travel

Close your eyes. Take a breath.

I invite you to join me in an exercise that my teacher and friend Akaya Windwood shares.

Imagine a descendant of yours, seven generations from now.

Picture this child. What are they wearing? Where are they? What are they doing?

Imagine this child thriving.

Take a breath.

Now open your eyes.

What can you do in this moment to ensure that your future descendants, *our* future descendants, thrive?

PRACTICE PROMPTS

Philanthropy Time Capsule

Imagine you are creating a time capsule with artifacts from your current giving. You can include strategy write-ups, budgets, dockets, and other materials that capture your current philanthropy. Reflect on how people finding your capsule twenty-five years, fifty years, and one hundred years from now will respond to your philanthropy.

What Time Is It?

Start your fundraising meetings, donor meetings, and board meetings with a question about how people are understanding these times. Invite multiple perspectives, and work toward aligning how funding organizations and the communities they serve understand the stakes and opportunities of our present moment.

Patience of a Thousand Years; Urgency of Now

Draw out these two intersecting circles on a large board. Put out pens for team members to write aspects of your organization's work in these circles, to visualize where it falls into this time spectrum. Reflect on what the completed circle is showing you and whether you want to make any adjustments.

Follow the Money

This moment demands a generous flow of capital into building a new, more just and equitable future. Yet most of philanthropy's work focuses on the minimum 5 percent payout foundations make as grants. This chapter offers a series of questions to unleash the impact of "the other 95 percent," the trillions of dollars in endowments and donor-advised funds that collectively have the potential to shape and incentivize a new and more just economy.

Years ago, I asked our foundation's investment advisers this question: How do we advance our commitment to racial, gender, and economic justice using our investments?

Their answers varied. In some cases, the question drew a deeply quizzical gaze, a long pause, a head scratch, and even a suspicion that I was asking a trick question. Other responses went quickly to diversity opportunities and a conversation about who manages funds and how we could incentivize changes in that arena.

A year later, I was still asking this question, but now we were in a different place. We had gathered more information, which we were beginning to apply to specific investments. Board members were beginning to ask similar and related questions. We updated our investment policy to reflect our commitment to racial and gender justice, and our investment decision-making criteria were now more aligned with our purpose. When our adviser recommended investment in "distressed debt," I now knew to ask, Who is in distress? Based on what we know about the rules of our economy, I knew to suspect that those in distress were likely disproportionately people of color. The act of asking these questions over time made room for new questions, new possibilities, new advisers, and new investment guidelines.

I love the advice that Angela Glover Blackwell, founder of PolicyLink, gave to a room of funders years ago: "Be the skunk at the garden party." Angela urged people to bring up the hard questions around equity—the ones that no one wants to discuss. We must get better at asking questions we don't fully know the answers to, while holding central to what we do know: our values and the missions that drive our work.

To support this practice, here are twenty questions for you to consider and discuss. These inquiries are designed to illuminate the next step in your journey of unleashing transformational impact with your assets.

1. In times of intersecting crises, what percentage of your capital are you deploying toward realizing your mission?

2. How do your investments reflect your values?

3. Is the organizational culture of your foundation more like an investment bank or financial institution, or like a nonprofit organization? Do you have elements of both within your organization? If yes, how do these cultures coexist and impact your ability to achieve your mission?

4. Are decisions and recommendations for grants and investments made using similar processes, with similar stakeholders, and with similar goals or outcomes in mind? If these processes differ, what assumptions underlie the difference in approach?

5. What might shift if the investments and grantmaking programs were more integrated?

6. Can you list three to five opportunities that exist to integrate investments with other foundation programs?

7. How does your organization define risk in your investment policy? Is it narrowly focused on the loss of capital, or does it include risks faced by grantees, communities, and future generations?

8. What risks can your foundation take that are distinct from those that other financial actors take?[1]

9. Does your organization seek a market rate return on investments? Why or why not?

10. How would you define a "fair" return on investments for foundations versus a "market return"?[2]

11. Who benefits the most from your endowment investments: the foundation or the community?

12. How might your capital be deployed in ways that shift how the economy operates?

13. Do your grantees or other community representatives have a voice or a stake in your investments?

14. Do your grantees and their communities have capital needs that go beyond the nonprofit model (grants) and are not likely to be funded through market forces? Are you investing in community-led models that are creating wealth, power, and justice?[3]

15. Are you investing in asset managers who understand and have a connection and commitment to your mission?

16. How are you catalyzing the creation of new investable opportunities by making your capital available, and your values and mission known?

17. How do you use your voice as an asset owner to speak out about policies and practices that harm communities and the planet?

18. In what forms will your foundation's capital (grant capital or investment capital) most quickly and effectively catalyze a more just and sustainable future?

19. Can you identify investments that conflict with or work against your programmatic goal? For example, are you a health funder who invests in big soda companies, a democracy funder invested in social media companies, or a funder concerned about climate change that is invested in fossil fuels?

20. What is the boldest and most aligned thing you could do with your investments in service of your grantees and the communities you support? What, specifically, is stopping you?

PRACTICE PROMPTS

The twenty questions above are designed to support investment committees and boards in having a rich dialogue and
identifying their next steps. You can use the questions to facilitate a discussion, or if you are looking for a more engaging
and fun way to approach this, try this activity:

Aligning Your Investments with Your Mission: Game Show Activity

1. You will need a notetaker and a host, who will ask the
   questions. Divide your investment committee or board
   into two teams.

2. The host will ask one of the questions from 1 to 17 above,
   and each team will have a chance to respond.

3. The host will give a point to the team that has the best
   answer. All answers will be captured by the notetaker.

4. The host will then do a bonus round, using questions 18,
   19, and 20. The best answers to each of these questions
   get double points.

5. The team with the most points gets a prize at the end.

6. Debrief as a full group about the conversation and pull
   out a few themes that the group would like to explore
   further, as well as two items for action. Share your lessons and insights with your peers.

Embody Change

How can we go from funding change to being the change? In this chapter, I highlight multiple ways that the concept of embodiment offers us a pathway to transformation as we build a new era of philanthropy.

One of the things I am learning about is embodiment as a portal to courage, wisdom, insight, and innovation. While there are many technical definitions of embodiment, I use the term here as a shorthand for the wisdom in this statement, popularly attributed to Gandhi, "Be the change you wish to see in the world." The key insight that embodiment offers is that the work of transformation isn't all "out there"; it also resides in us.

A rarely spoken truth is that many of us working in institutional philanthropy remain in our heads, where our fears and anxieties cloud our sense of possibility. The notion of embodiment is in many ways the opposite of the heady and cerebral philanthropic cultures and norms. So much of the valued labor in our sector is about thinking big thoughts. Philanthropy prizes expressions of intelligence that are familiar in legal and academic settings and downplays the value of other forms of wisdom. Our love language is the well-argued memo. Philanthropic culture often values academic knowledge over embodied lived experience.

I am not an expert on embodiment. And yet I know that in this new era of philanthropy, somatic skills and an attention to embodied experience are an essential component of making transformational change. To transform the world around us, we too must transform. When we live in unequal systems, these systems also live in us, and if we are not intentional, we risk re-creating these unequal systems through our philanthropy. When we bring an awareness to what we are embodying, we can begin the work of slowly but surely embodying the future we seek. In this chapter, I ask, as funders, what do we embody? Are we embodying our origins in systems of extraction, or our values and the more just future we seek to fund? How might embodiment help us show up with more courage and wisdom?

I write this chapter as a student who is learning about what it takes for us to show up fully in our work to build more liberated futures. When it comes to embodiment practices, I lift up and honor experts like Prentis Hemphill, Staci K. Haines, Eveline Shen, and others who have deep expertise and practice in bringing these tools to people who are working to transform systems. I also honor leaders like Dr. Yanique Redwood, who reminds us that the toll of this work is experienced differently by specific bodies.

Going Forward Together

As a leader, Eveline Shen is often described as grounded and purposeful, two characteristics that no doubt come from her embodiment practices. I first met Eveline in 2010 when she was leading Forward Together, a reproductive justice organization. The staff at Forward Together, like so many other social change organizations, were skilled in policy advocacy, communications, and movement building. They were also deeply skilled at something very different: embodiment.

At Forward Together, the team began each day with a practice that Eveline learned from working with Norma Wong of the Institute for Applied Zen—a mix of tai chi–inspired movements, breath, and voice. Eveline continued to build out the practice to help activists step into their leadership and build alignment. Eveline explained that each element of the practice was an opportunity to embody the change they were seeking: "Social justice work is inherently about movement. It's about change. And there's a physical component to the process of organizing, building movement, and shifting power."[1] Using their voices helped them speak loudly and clearly together; moving their bodies in unison helped them move their strategies together.

As a Forward Together board member, and later as a funder of their work, I witnessed how critical this embodied practice was to the organization's broader impact. As Eveline shared, practicing Forward Stance as a group "provided us with a powerful way to learn and gain new insight through physical movement and by reconnecting our bodies with our minds."[2]

Over time, Eveline integrated this mind-body practice into the Courageous Operating System, to help "leaders navigate through challenging situations and achieve a meaningful, sustainable, and impactful life while making deep change on the individual, community, and movement levels."[3] In her training on the Courageous Operating System, she includes a physical practice to help people physically embody what it is like to hold conflict together, balancing their own experiences at the same time as those of their partner. In addition, by integrating music into these trainings, Eveline helps leaders not only find the power in their voices but also use their voices together in a way that promotes harmony, beauty, and healing.

Practices of embodiment are not new. In many communities, embodiment practices are a pathway to reclaiming indigenous wisdom and cultural practices in communities of color. Forward Together is in good company with many social justice organizations that have incorporated somatic practices into their transformation work. National Domestic Workers Alliance, Black Organizing for Leadership and Dignity (BOLD), and generative somatics are a few of the organizations that use strategies of embodiment as part of their broader transformation strategies.

In the early weeks of the pandemic, Eveline brought the Courageous Operating System to a set of twenty funders in a series of online virtual meetings. She encouraged us to move together, breathe together, and even sing together as we grappled with how best to lead in uncertain times. Her hope in offering these practices was that if funders could be integrated in mind and body, we could lead in more courageous ways. With her offering, Eveline invited funders to tap into a broader set of intelligences, so we could show up in the ways that our community partners needed.

It was these sessions that helped me find my courage in the early weeks of the pandemic to make a bold funding request to my board—a request that I knew would upset at least one powerful member.

As I prepared to request increased funding from my board, I breathed. I slowed down. I remembered that our bodies have a capacity for discomfort, and that discomfort wasn't a reason to hold back on what was needed in that time.

Our assets were down dramatically, and yet I wanted to ask our board not only to increase our spending but to do so for three years. It was in the early weeks of the pandemic, and funders were already revising and reducing their grants budgets, in a moment in which grantee needs were greater than ever. As I had shared in an op-ed, even in the early weeks of COVID-19, the pandemic was showing us that power is literally a matter of life and death:

> The heart of this crisis is all about power: who is heard, whose interests are protected, who is afforded agency over their lives and livelihoods. What is really called for in this time is a long-term, large-scale philanthropic response to shift power to people and support organizations in building a just and caring society.[4]

Stepping into the discomfort, I asked my board to dramatically increase our payout. When I centered and slowed down, I could see that it was my responsibility to share my best wisdom in that moment with my trustees. They met my embodied request with a resounding yes.

How Does Philanthropy Feel? On Discomfort

If you pay close attention to the op-ed pages of the philanthropic media, you might notice that one of the biggest insults that can be lobbed at a philanthropic approach is that it is "feel-good." If this critique were used to name the dynamic of gilded philanthropy—giving that follows exploitation—it might be a fitting description of how philanthropy is used to make a donor feel good about themselves. But where this phrase is used more often is to describe philanthropy that moves away from control and compliance orientations and is more trust-based and relational. "Feel-good" philanthropy is held up as the opposite of "rigorous" metric-driven philanthropy. It has a gendered connotation to it, with donors like MacKenzie Scott portrayed as "feel-good" while donors like Bill Gates are seen as "strategic."

This phrase always makes me wonder: How do we *think* funding is supposed to feel? In this new era of philanthropy, where we are shifting both power and resources, those of us who are moving resources should feel some amount of discomfort. After all, change, transition, and transformation are all processes that require us to move from the relative comfort of the status quo into something new; that can be uncomfortable! And yet, if we are working in this context of so much power and privilege, we can learn to see the discomfort as an indicator that we are on the right track. That nervous feeling in your belly could be a somatic sign of you forging the philanthropy we need in these times.

We can also learn to do this together. When we gather, let's share our stories of the most uncomfortable moments we've had in our work recently. Stitched together, these stories will be of a new philanthropy that emerges when we are willing to hold the discomfort inherent in transitions and shake loose embodied and outdated ways of holding power and wealth.

How Does Philanthropy Feel? On Joy

Here is a related, and in many ways more important, question: How does it *really* feel to get funding? When I've been a grant recipient, I've experienced a range of feelings. On rare occasions, I've had the pleasure of feeling true partnership and full possibility, the feeling of someone truly believing in you and your abilities. I have literally jumped up and down with glee after getting an email saying yes to a funding request. There is an expansiveness and a space of possibility that can open in that feeling of partnership.

But usually getting funding feels stressful. So many grantee leaders have shared over the years that working with funders is the hardest part of their jobs. I have felt that too: It can feel like a constant exercise in navigating power, where you are told, not asked. It can feel like you have to always say yes or risk losing funding—yes to every invitation to speak, every coffee, every survey, every request to "pick your brain." The way that power plays out in funding relationships is that many grant recipients feel like they can't say no to a funder's request, no matter how unreasonable.

An executive director described how it feels to engage with funders in this way: "The pull to abuse power when you are in philanthropy is very strong. And I don't mean in nefarious, malicious ways. I mean in the everyday microaggression ways that being a person who has the power to decide where money goes can spawn abuse."[5]

It is important to note that how it feels isn't always a product of whether the answer to a funding request is a yes or no. Skillful funders say no with integrity, partnership, an explanation, and even an offering, like constructive feedback or an introduction to another funder. The explanation can create more understanding about the ecosystem in which the funder and grantee sit, so the feeling is that we are building toward a similar future, even if we are not in a funding relationship.

"What does it feel like?" is the question I had in mind when we kicked off our grant application redesign process at General Service Foundation. Rather than beginning with any number of standard goals, I wanted us to begin with this question: How does it feel to apply for our funding?

The team gathered in a conference room. We began our process by remembering how we felt at different times when applying for funding. One of our program officers was a past grantee of the foundation. She described how "seen" she felt by the program officer who had responded to her cold email and had taken care in learning about her work. She also remembered the nerves she felt when she met her program officer for the first time. I shared a time when the process of applying for funding sharpened the strategy I was leading, and another time that a funder affirmed and believed in a big strategic shift we were making—and how amazing that felt. We all remember times when a grant process felt stressful, disconnected, extractive, and insulting.

We concluded that the answer to this question—How do we want grantees to feel as they apply for funding?—was joyful.

It felt ambitious and clarifying. As we redesigned and streamlined our grants process, we had "joyful" as our goal post. When our new grants application launched, we included a few questions to assess what it felt like for grantees. Based on what we heard, it wasn't joyful, but it was "easeful." Our central question, and the attention we placed on the grantee experience, led us to this place of progress.

In this new era, funders are investing in joy as a strategy for liberation. In 2022, the Disability Inclusion Fund launched "joy grants": $10,000 in unrestricted funds "to expand the capacity of [disability-led] community organizations to rest and reflect on movement strategies, strengthen and foster community relationship-building, and support access to collective life-affirming experiences."[6] The Disability Inclusion Fund recognized that investing in joy was central to collective liberation and Disability Justice principles of sustainability and wholeness. Joy grants highlight that grantees are often forced to choose between resourcing strategies and giving staff a necessary opportunity to rest and reconnect. Sandy Ho, who launched joy grants and is the former director of the Disability Inclusion Fund, shared that "the hope is that by incorporating this practice, others in philanthropy will understand that movement work has an emotional, mental, and physical toll year after year, and that investing in rest and joy is critical to our collective liberation and long-term movement goals."[7]

When asked how funders could reshape their grantmaking practices to better resource disabled-led joy, one grantee responded,

> It's a sense of freedom in orientation. If grantmaking is just about keeping the lights on, surviving, meeting basic needs, or checking off each concrete goal, then the magic that occurs when joy is allowed to enter the space is lost. People tend to thrive when oriented to joy; joy engenders creativity. But it's also the whole point. We want disabled people to lead full, joyful lives.

We live in high-stakes, chaotic, and stressful times. I want philanthropy to feel like an act of joy, solidarity, and mutuality. What if we agreed that philanthropy is not only supposed to be "feel-good," but that it should feel good? Like a dance party—kinetic, collaborative, joyful, with lots of mirroring and a lot less control. There should be rhythm and so much movement.

Embodying the More Just Future

Philanthropy often approaches change and transformation as if it is something that happens outside the doors of the foundation, outside of us. Rarely do we see our philanthropic institutions for what they could be: sites of experimentation and practice for more equitable and just approaches. If foundations are part of a larger ecosystem that's pushing for new and more equitable practices, we can be resource-rich sites for practicing and experimenting with these new norms.

I'll share an example. A decade ago, as I sought to create a forward-thinking policy on family leave, I called my fellow foundation leaders who were funding reproductive justice work. My assumption was that they would share examples of values-aligned policies reflecting their organizations' commitment to reproductive justice. Instead, I was surprised to learn that some foundations had no policy, whereas others had policies that reflected the legal minimums.

To draft the leave policy, I sought the input of Sarita Gupta, a labor organizer, codirector of Caring Across Generations, executive director of Jobs with Justice, and GSF board member. In the field, Sarita was advocating for policy and culture change that centers care. Her expertise helped us draft a policy that aligned with our values and reflected norms that may not have been widely adopted yet, but that we knew would be part of the future we were working toward. Our new policy offered six months of paid leave to new parents and twelve weeks of paid leave to care for a sick family member.

Our new family leave policy made it possible for staff members to step into caretaking roles at critical moments in their lives. And it had impacts beyond that. The process of creating a new policy and having our board approve it created a deeper understanding and buy-in into the future we were trying to fund. It made abstract notions like care, thriving, and flourishing tactile and concrete because we were creating the kind of policy that would be the norm in a society that centers care. By aligning our values with our policies, we were joining others beyond our organization in demonstrating that it is possible for employers to create policies that center care.

Affirmatively embodying the future is a practice for leaning against embodied gilded defaults from the past. In philanthropy, these defaults include the practices and cultures that have led to an accumulation of wealth, capital, and power for the few. As I think about this transition that we are in, I imagine a stage in which philanthropy and the organizations we fund are understood to be sites for practicing and experimenting more broadly with the new norms we are working toward.

Whose Bodies?

As a woman of color who has spent her career in the elite and mostly white spaces of law and philanthropy, I have an almost unconscious habit of counting the people of color in a room when I walk into it. This habit likely developed early in my career when I was often the only woman of color in a room, and sometimes the only woman at a table. Thankfully this phenomenon has changed dramatically in recent years.

In 2019, when I was a speaker at a conference, I recall feeling such joy and belonging when I walked into a room filled with women of color. It felt like a moment that I had longed for in the sector, and it gave me chills. But the ecstatic feeling didn't last long. I took my seat and then listened over the next few hours to this room full of powerful leaders describing in painful detail the shared feeling of disempowerment, of feeling unseen and unheard in their roles. Their stories made my stomach hurt with a sinking feeling of recognition. Their voices stayed with me for weeks. Across institutions, these leaders were saying, we don't feel welcome; we don't feel like we belong.

How can we bring an embodied approach to this work when we feel like our bodies are not welcome and do not belong in this sector? In 2020, after the murder of George Floyd, a critical mass of foundations began engaging in reflective processes to examine who gets to do the work of philanthropy in their institutions. There was a more robust effort to remove some of the long-standing barriers that have kept people of color, trans and queer people, and people with disabilities from having a seat at the table. Yet this commitment to equity has ebbed and flowed. After the 2023 Supreme Court ruling limiting affirmative action programs in higher education, and the US Court of Appeals for the 11th Circuit 2024 ruling that blocked the Fearless Fund from making grants to Black Women entrepreneurs, some foundations have started to quietly abandon both racial justice grantmaking and efforts to build a more inclusive philanthropy.[8]

Every day, our bodies work in a sector defined by power. Breathing, moving, scanning, sitting, and experiencing our roles, our work, and our days in ways that are impacted by who we are. When I first began working in professional philanthropy, very few institutions were led by women of color. It was not unusual for these mostly male, mostly white leaders to enjoy long tenures of two to three decades in their roles. Because few of these foundation leaders had connections to or were shaped by the communities they served, many defaulted to roles, especially in family foundations, that were understood as being of service to a wealthy family. My observation is that these leaders saw protection as part of their roles—protecting the endowment assets from risk, and protecting the wealthy donors from discomfort.

This model of foundation leadership, focused on the comfort of those with wealth and power, is of the past gilded philanthropy. I belong to a new generation of leaders of color who have diversified the leadership of professional philanthropy. The shift underway isn't just about different bodies; it is a much broader and more fundamental shift. Many of us see ourselves as being in service to movements and communities, not to a particular family. In our work with donors and families, our service is a leadership approach that supports wealthy donors in learning and evolving their understanding of how all our futures are tied and interdependent. Many of us see our role as bridging and facilitating the evolution that is needed as we move into this next era of philanthropy. The work of bridging is so needed, and it can be fraught and difficult work, especially in cultures where exclusion and hierarchies persist.

Dr. Yanique Redwood provides a window into how exclusion impacts our bodies in her book *White Women Cry & Call Me Angry*. A former

CEO of a health conversion foundation, she chronicles how working in the white-dominant culture of philanthropy destroyed her health, and her journey back to healing and joy. As she describes her journey to transform the institution she led into an antiracist organization, she chronicles the resistance she was met with and how that felt in her body: "I want to make it clear that racism matters for health, mental health, maternal health, and longevity."[9]

Redwood's story resonates with the many stories told in the spring 2024 issue of *Nonprofit Quarterly* in an article titled "Stop Drowning Us, and Stop Making Us Disappear: A Critical Report on the State of Black Woman Leadership." Cyndi Suarez, editor in chief of *Nonprofit Quarterly*, says in her letter from the editor, "There is no place allowed, it seems, to breathe; to rest; to grow; to make mistakes, learn, and recalibrate; to be. The sector, as a number of leaders describe in this edition, is perpetrating death by a thousand cuts."[10]

It is hard for me to imagine how we meet the challenges of these times without creating new cultures of true belonging. And yet, too many of us who step up and step into the challenges of leadership find ourselves in Andrew Carnegie's philanthropy. What we are building in this new era of philanthropy is space for so many more of us to belong and lead and shape a philanthropy that serves our communities. Until we get there, and I know we will, we must understand the toll that othering has on our bodies.

Carrying These Times in Our Bodies

When I worked as a legal services lawyer, my colleagues and I represented people living through the worst moments in their lives: losing their jobs, homes, and even custody of their children. While representing them, we sometimes experienced vicarious, or secondary, trauma by virtue of proximity to people experiencing acute trauma. Vicarious trauma can lead to feelings of overwhelm, compassion fatigue, health issues, and a desire to avoid work interactions with clients. When I moved from working at a legal services organization to a philanthropic one, I noted how the relative distance that funders have from the front lines made vicarious trauma a rare phenomenon.

More recently, though, as we have been living through times of "recurrent crises and chaotic conditions,"[11] I've started to notice signs that resemble vicarious trauma in philanthropy. I first noticed it when we shifted our reporting practice from written reports to a phone call check-in. I recall a program officer coming to me at the end of the day, describing how multiple grantees had broken down in tears during their calls. It was early in the first Trump administration, and so many of our grantee partners were overwhelmed by all the fires and attacks on their communities. My colleague had the superpower of empathy, and after these calls, I would see in her some of the trauma markers that I had seen so often as a lawyer.

Whether or not this is a form of trauma, I recognize the toll that many people who are working toward a more just future are carrying in their bodies. I am curious about how our positionality in philanthropy shapes the toll of this work. Institutional philanthropy has been described as taking the "thirty-thousand-foot view"—seeing connections between and across issues, but never close enough to touch down. Not proximate, but instead high up and with a long view.

As we move toward an approach to funding where we are building relationships of partnership, proximity, and accountability, this hierarchical model of funders at the top is less useful and less accurate. In this new era of philanthropy, I think of philanthropy's positionality as highly networked, where we are steeped in relationships and information that help us spot emergent patterns and crises.

It is our job as funders to be attuned to shifting conditions. I saw the toll of this positionality in 2020, as we approached the election. Several of us were sounding the alarm about the possibilities of vigilantism, violence, and other "not normal" things that we had not seen in generations. Our highly networked positionality meant that we could clearly see the difficult things that were coming: attacks on our democracy, climate crisis, and increased fractures in our civic body.

In times of crisis, our positionality as proximate funders can lead to fatigue, numbing, and overwhelm. That we are more proximate is an encouraging sign that we are moving toward sharing power with grantees. And yet, it comes with this increase in shared trauma. As we evolve our positionality, we must take greater care to look for the signs of this in our bodies, our spirits, and our work—and engage in supportive practices that address the toll of this work in these times.

Grounding in Our Bodies

I've noticed these days that so many of us are holding our breath. At conferences, speakers talk about intersecting, compounding, and escalating crises, and I rub my temples, feeling a migraine coming on. Their voices are tight as they say, "These times are urgent!" They are right, of course, but I look around and I wonder if our bodies and minds have learned how to process the multiple fires. And are we all okay as we juggle existential emergencies with writing memos and making dinner for the kids?

Some of us respond to crises with frenetic activity. We want so badly to just do something, to be responsive, to move fast. And so there is lots of activity and lots of running around, and after some time, it takes its toll on our bodies. Others respond to crises by going numb or freezing, like deer in the headlights. Activity slows down and responsiveness drops away.

I've fallen into the frenetic activity camp, but after spending much of my adult life in head-first professions, I no longer believe that we can solve things in a dissociated way. I am learning to approach crises from a place of grounding. When I start a call now, I like to do so by taking a few breaths together. In moments of stress, I invite people to feel into their bodies, to feel their breath filling their bellies. When building an agenda for a group, I pay as much attention to downtime as programmed time—spaces for connection, relationship-building, and being present. These small ways of coming into and staying in our bodies change our experience and how we show up. When we are embodied, we can choose not to be frenetic, or slow, but rather to be integrated, body and mind, and to move with others from a place of wisdom to meet the moment.

PRACTICE PROMPTS

Mapping Joy and Discomfort

Host a storytelling circle about how philanthropy feels. Create a visual map and note patterns and trends in the actions that create joy, discomfort, and other feelings.

Building Your Toolkit

Make a list of the tools and practices you can personally draw on to stay embodied in times of change and crisis. What helps you navigate discomfort?

Getting Out of Our Heads

Introduce movement and embodied practices at staff and board meetings. Take five-minute breaks to allow for stretching, walking, and dancing. In moments of tension, invite people to return to their breath and their bodies. Note how these practices shift the work.

Identify and Replace Philanthropic Artifacts

The methods of philanthropic practice—the nuts and bolts we've put in place to "do" philanthropy—often create barriers for nonprofits and community-serving groups to do their work. This chapter examines gilded philanthropy norms for how funders decide what to do (strategy) and how to measure it (evaluation) along with stories and examples of how new era funders are replacing these artifacts with approaches that are responsive to our times.

In late 2023, the *New York Times* Styles Desk team gathered to discuss the rerelease of one of my favorite shows from childhood, *LA Law. New York Times* editors Minju Pak and Jim Windolf were also fans back in the day and wanted to hear the responses of their younger colleagues when the show became available for viewing for the first time in forty years.[1]

My relationship with *LA Law* is nostalgic: While I can't recall any specific episodes, I do remember impressions of a thrilling and glamorous depiction of adult office life. Reading about the show as seen through fresh eyes, and as described by the Millennial and Gen Z journalists Jim Windolf and reporter Louis Lucero II, made me laugh until I cried, and provided new insights:

LOUIS LUCERO II: In spite of myself, there was a lot that I found delightful. It's *always* intoxicating to see an analog office, for starters—the visual equivalent of ASMR for the Slack-addled millennial brain.

JIM WINDOLF: It's hard to imagine what people did in their offices when there's no computer on the desk.

LL: People running around with manila envelopes and little slips of paper that say who called? Literally unimaginable. Too cute for words! Did people *realize* how adorable they were being?

JW: They did not.

Lucero goes on to describe the show as "an artifact. A trapped-in-amber, predictably problematic, genuinely funny artifact." Of course the offices of 1984 look odd to those watching today. They are filled with strange artifacts that no longer make sense—desks without computers?

The review hilariously captures the simple truth that as time passes, norms shift. Things we long took for granted as unalterable eventually stop making sense as contexts change. This is an apt description for so much of philanthropic practice: It is an artifact, out of step with the times.

Our sensibilities and needs change. In this new era of philanthropy, funders and communities may look back at today's philanthropy and say, "Literally unimaginable."

Excavating New Possibilities

This chapter explores two of the most fundamental and soon to be relics of modern giving: how funders approach philanthropic strategy and evaluation. For each, I share stories and examples from the field. My goal is not an exhaustive treatment of strategy and evaluation, but rather to inspire more funders to examine today's norms and recognize the opportunities we have to transform these artifacts into approaches that are more responsive, impactful, and aligned with community needs.

I offer reflections on how we can transform today's strategy and evaluation artifacts into powerful approaches that support changemakers:

- Instead of funders adopting a "wait and see" approach, do and learn.

- Build strategies rooted in the real world, not just on paper or in fiction.

- Be prepared—by letting values, right role, flexibility, and emergent strategies lead.

- Reframe strategy as values, and ensure that you have strategic muscles and mind-sets.

- Understand that real accountability flows two ways.

- Know your evaluation "why."

- Learn to trust ourselves and each other.

Instead of Wait and See, Do and Learn

The election of President Donald Trump in November 2016 was a moment that changed everything. Trump had campaigned on a brand of misogyny, racism, and xenophobia. Many of us woke up on the morning of November 9, 2016, clear that progress toward equity and justice was not only in peril but that we were going into a time in which the government would be used as a powerful tool to attack so many of our communities.

In my conversations with nonprofit and community leaders in the weeks that followed, they all shared some version of two thoughts: First, leaders knew that the world had changed and that the needs of their communities were about to expand dramatically. They understood that to meet these growing needs, their work would have to evolve and they would need additional resources. They worried that in this new, openly hostile environment, it would no longer be possible to do the work of keeping communities safe and their rights protected in the same way.

Second, they feared losing funding. In this changed context, the deliverables spelled out in current grants either no longer applied or were no longer possible. Our partners were on the front lines, working on gender, reproductive justice, and immigrant rights. The stakes were incredibly high. Leaders expressed little confidence in philanthropy's ability to understand the gravity of this moment and fund accordingly. But I reassured them that funders were bound to understand the profoundly altered environment and respond with increased flexibility and additional resources.

But that's not what happened. Instead, as we moved into 2017, and nonprofits found themselves facing a firehose of regressive and discriminatory policies (the Muslim ban, separating children from their parents at the border, and numerous attacks on workers' rights and protections), many funders retreated into strategic planning. The reason? Their existing strategic plans made less sense given the new moment. As organizations sought additional funding for urgently needed capacities, they found a philanthropic field that was frozen, and their requests were met with versions of, "We don't know what's going to happen, so it's important to take a wait-and-see approach."

The swift rise of Trumpism unraveled decades of civil rights progress. Few funding strategies anticipated this shift, and too few funders pivoted quickly to support a radically changed landscape. Having a giving strategy is key. But it shouldn't require eighteen months to figure out—not if we are clear about who we are, what we believe, and where we're heading. And especially not when the world clock is ticking.

This wait-and-see approach to strategy is a philanthropic artifact because it prioritizes the funder's desire to maintain order, keep the status quo, and know all the facts before responding over responding to the real and urgent needs in communities. Funders can afford to wait and see because they are less likely to feel the immediate impact of a changed environment. This ability to wait is, in its own way, a luxury. The uncertainty that funders experience when things shift also stems from not having directly impacted people represented enough in philanthropic spaces. I can recall being at a board meeting of the foundation I led a few days after the 2016 election. It was the people of color in the room who already had stories about what this election would mean—its effect was already rippling through our communities. The board's culture, which leaned toward learning, curiosity, and humility, created a container in which it was our experiences that shaped the organization's desire to be responsive.

To meet the challenges of these times, instead of waiting and seeing, we must do and learn (and do and learn and do and learn). Our strategies must move at the speed of these times, and match, or at least honor, the dynamism and urgency that characterize the work of our nonprofit partners.

Build Strategies Rooted in Real-World Feedback

Most funders have been taught to create funding strategies based on a few *(false)* assumptions:

1. Social change is linear and predictable *(it isn't)*.

2. A strategic plan means we, as funders, can control what will happen, including dictating the outcomes we desire *(it won't)*.

3. The more planning we do, the more we will know what to do should things change *(definitely not)*.

Many funding strategies contain a fiction at their heart: If I fund X, then Y will happen, based on very reasonable logic models. If only the world were so contained and neat! In reality, both social change and the context in which social change occurs are far more messy, dynamic, and unpredictable than most strategies account for.

Yet, it is standard or even considered best practice in philanthropy for funders to conduct painfully slow strategic planning processes. Many organizations hire expensive firms to shepherd them along a lengthy process, at the end of which they are handed a prescription. Strategies may differ in detail, but the format is often the same: a detailed slide deck, with logic models, accountability rubrics, and annual benchmarks. The amount of resources that go into these efforts is staggering, not to mention hundreds of hours of staff and board time. Strategic planning firms are establishing industry norms around what is important and who holds knowledge, and community voices are rarely centered in these processes.

There's something broken in how we understand what it means to have a strategy. A foundation's strategic plan must be different than a nonprofit's strategic plan because their roles are different. Most often, foundations are not directly engaged in the work they are funding, and so their plans must reflect their role. Too often, foundations put together strategic plans that can only be successful if their grantees execute the foundation's goals, not necessarily their own. The strategic plan then is only achievable if funders engage in a level of constant control over grantee partners. This control takes us right back to gilded philanthropy—remember Carnegie's book about what he wanted to see in the libraries?

Here is an example: A large foundation seeks to solve the problem of homelessness. Most advocates would tell you that this is a complex issue and one that requires interventions at multiple levels in multiple systems. The risk here is that as the funder maps out their strategy, they are setting the strategy for the field by deciding which approaches they will resource and which they won't. Funders are rarely best positioned to make those calls, because their positionality is less proximate than the advocates who are working on this issue and seeing the daily complexities of it.

Philanthropic strategy must start with clarity about the funder's right role. The role of funders is to resource, and to be flexible and responsive to the needs of communities and nonprofits, who must make their own strategic choices based on their expertise and proximity.

Too often, foundations' strategic plans do not map onto how social change happens in the real world. Instead, they place far too much importance on the role of the foundation and its funding, and far too little importance on the complexity and significance of everything else. Yet internally, these documents are often treated as sacrosanct. So invested are we in these labor- and resource-intensive processes that we allow them to dictate what is and isn't possible, regardless of what is happening outside our doors.

A few years ago, when I walked into the Ford Foundation, I saw a wall-size printout of a *New Yorker* cartoon. The image was of two men, one smiling with his head out the window throwing dollar bills to the world below, and the other saying with concern, "Just a minute, young man. That's not quite the way we do things here at the Ford Foundation."

"Just a minute, young man. That's not quite the way
we do things here at the Ford Foundation."

Source: *Robert J. Day/The New Yorker Collection/The Cartoon Bank;* © *Condé Nast*

I love this cartoon, first because as funders we don't often get to laugh at ourselves, but also because it perfectly illustrates a false narrative between the typical strategic approach (If you don't have a long, drawn-out strategic planning process, you're doing it wrong!) and the perception that the alternative is: You have no strategy.

I think we could benefit from a second cartoon: The world is burning, the waters are rising, the pandemic is spreading; community members are trying to help one another to safety. Two nonprofit leaders are in the crowd, which has gathered outside the foundation's office. One turns to the other and asks, "Where are the funders?" The second figure points up at a window and replies, "Oh, they're still in strategic planning."

Move from Having a Strategy to Being Strategic

In my early months at GSF, I could see that our work would be more impactful if we had a clearer organizational strategy. Every program officer and board member I talked to seemed to be describing a different foundation, each with its own priorities. Speaking with staff and board members, I listened deeply to understand. What are we trying to do as an organization? What's our collective goal? And how could we move out of our silos to work toward collaborative goals?

Intending to identify the North Star of our work, we embarked on a process to clarify our organizational strategy. Rather than developing a strategic plan, I invested instead in our organization's capacity *to think and act strategically.* We worked with Eugene Eric Kim, from Faster Than 20, who introduced us to the concept and process of building "muscles and mind-sets" to strengthen our ability to be strategic and collaborative to achieve shared goals.[2]

Eugene approached strategy as a muscle that could be built, and so our staff and board went through a boot camp of sorts, with weekly exercises that helped us all build the skill set around strategic decision-making and action. This shared work also helped us deepen our relationships with one another. There were different frameworks in the room, different lived experiences and political orientations, and these weekly conversations allowed us to build a shared culture.

The hours of conversation and relationship-building went into cocreating something useful and foundational for our organization: a North Star for our work. Our values and vision fit on a single 8½-by-11 page. This was different from strategic plans that I had been part of in past organizations, long documents that eventually gathered dust on bookshelves. This document was a living strategic purpose that we as staff and board created together and sought to embody, one that would become a compass for our future work. We identified justice as our North Star, we clarified a set of organizational beliefs and values that encompassed our vision of justice. The vision was informed by deep listening to our grantees and their experiences. Not only did this relational process help us align the institution, but we were stronger for it, because we had built trust and connection.

Weeks later, when President Trump was elected and the world as we knew it changed, our team had what we needed to lead our organization in ways that were responsive to community needs. Whereas embarking on a strategic planning process might have slowed us down and held us back, clarity on our shared organizational values and vision gave us a runway and space to be bold and move in partnership with our grantees as things changed rapidly.

A Values-Based Approach to Strategy

The "best" strategic plan does not ensure that your organization will engage in strategic funding. Moving strategically takes more than a plan: It requires a set of skills, frameworks, and organizational infrastructure that promote strategic action.

How might we be better grantmakers if we invested more time and resources into understanding what is at stake in the present moment, rather than trying to guess what might be relevant two, three, or five years into the future? While funders tend to be removed from community-level change, our nonprofit partners often are not. When we engage with grantees and really listen, we can get a better sense of how conditions are shifting, and with those changes, how what they need from funders is changing.

Additionally, while external conditions are always shifting, what we believe—our core values and our mission—tends to be more solid and fixed. Our beliefs are a more precise guide for action than plans that may quickly become outdated. Foundation leaders can be prepared for what might come next when we are clear on our beliefs and understand what matters most to us, so that our institutions know how to act.

How can we be strategic without going offline and into strategic planning whenever things change? I want to offer a different approach, rooted in values. The stakes and possibilities of these times require strategies that are values-first, right-role, flexible, and emergent:

Values-first. Funding strategies must start with having clarity about the kind of world we are trying to help build. Knowing what matters to us allows us to know when and how we must take action. This provides an essential context and purpose for all our work.

Many foundations have a list of values on their websites. The ask here is that we embody our values—that we understand our values as being aspirations we are living into in all corners of our institution. When we approach values this way, we can bring them into every decision we make. When we understand values as something we do, not just something we say, it helps us move a strategy from a theory into something we are practicing in the real world. You know you are living into your values when they are referenced and raised in investment strategies, grant allocations, spending decisions, and hiring processes.

It is also important to note that we live in times in which values have become political. Values of equity and belonging are being contested, legislated, and limited in our politics, and political parties are running on campaigns that build bases through strategies of othering and dehumanizing people. Knowing our values in these times means being willing to stand up for these values, even when, and especially when, they are politicized.

Right-role. A funder's primary role is to deploy resources. As we develop strategies, we must make sure they are complementary to but distinct from work that can only be done by grantees. When funders map their strategies directly onto grantees' strategies, their role becomes one of control, monitoring, and enforcement.

Flexible. We must develop approaches that are flexible and responsive, rather than rigid and rooted in control. None of us know how things will unfold by looking into a glass ball. Yet we know things will change, and that our responses in those moments will be increasingly consequential and have a real impact on people's lives.

Emergent. An emergent approach is iterative: You learn and apply lessons, things shift and change, you try new things and learn some more, and so on. As funders, our role is to keep doing and learning, in partnership with the field. With an emergent approach, we don't assume we know everything, or that we can control anything. We can reject the false certainty and some of the ego of strategic philanthropy and instead acknowledge that we are working within complex, ever-changing systems.

It would be a missed opportunity to use the word *emergent* in the context of strategy and not lift up adrienne maree brown's masterpiece *Emergent Strategy*. The scope of *Emergent Strategy* goes well beyond the ways I use *emergent* here, but I highly recommend the book to anyone who wants to "radically change the world." One piece of wisdom from brown's book is her focus on the relationships and connection in the context of strategy:

> Emergence emphasizes critical connections over critical mass, building authentic relationships, listening with all the senses of the body and the mind.[3]

Know Your Evaluation "Why"

Strategic plans often are followed by evaluation and measurement. It is hard to overstate how burdensome philanthropic evaluation processes can be on nonprofit partners. Grantees are routinely asked to provide different metrics to different funders for similar work because each funder is measuring their own unique set of metrics. The current approach to evaluation is resource- and labor-intensive and offers little value to grantee partners. In other words, it's an artifact just waiting to be cataloged.

I have seen philanthropic evaluation and measurement approaches slow down progress, time and again. A peer foundation president called me in 2020, concerned about their democracy funding. His program team told him they were hearing from field leaders that they needed money to challenge the increased voter suppression they were seeing. The foundation's democracy strategy was to invest in efforts to reach individual voters. While the two seem related to anyone scanning the page, the foundation had built an elaborate evaluation metric to count each voter that their grantees made contact with. The challenge? Efforts to challenge voter suppression were not countable in their existing rubric.

Speaking about his staff, he said, "I know they're right. The field needs resources to battle voter suppression. But I just don't know how we can fund that. We built our evaluation metrics and strategy around the number of voters our funding helps to turn out—not the number of voters who are suppressed."

My peer felt pressure from his board to remain accountable to the strategy, even though it was no longer the most relevant need, even though he saw the direct threat to democracy if he couldn't find a way to pivot. He knew organizations on the ground needed support fighting voter suppression and strengthening democracy, the foundation's overarching goal, but he felt stuck to the original strategy. The metric won.

As a sector, we have learned to put our faith in our strategic plans and metrics rather than in ourselves and the people we hire to act strategically. This level of disconnect between our plans to move resources to communities getting in the way of moving them has created a kind of accountability charade. In this scenario, we've removed agency and responsibility from people who work at foundations and put the plans in charge.

There are many more stories like this that prove that it's possible and all too common to lose sight of our work and goals when our evaluation strategies are not rooted in a wider "why." For example: The short periods of time funders use to measure change miss the longer-term effects of our investments. Or how funders measure how grantee partners furthered the foundation's strategy, not their own strategy. Or how foundations narrowly measure the impact of our own grants as if they exist in isolation from all other investments.

Measuring and Evaluating Versus Learning

In this new era, we can revisit our approaches to evaluation and learning, and bring a clearer purpose and intention to this work. It is worth asking if our current evaluation efforts are truly furthering our learning. I recently supported a large foundation in integrating trust-based approaches into their grantmaking. The foundation had an elaborately detailed strategy and a set of over a hundred metrics that they measured internally to assess progress on their strategy. Staff throughout the foundation tracked and contributed to these metrics. As the foundation looked for ways to incorporate more streamlined processes, they kept running into the barrier of these metrics. It came out that even though there was support among the foundation leadership for moving to a more manageable and less metrics-driven learning framework, some staff were reluctant to let go of the cumbersome metrics, because the metrics were serving a function of helping staff be seen in this large organization. This was a reminder to me that sometimes, our evaluation metrics serve internal and cultural purposes that are not about learning.

In other settings, metrics are used to make a case about the foundation's own relevance and impact—data is used to tell a story that makes the foundation, and perhaps their trustees, feel good about their work. Metrics are also seen as a tool that promotes accountability. At one foundation a staff member explained sincerely, "Our metrics are fundamentally how we stay accountable to the community. We are entrusted by the community to oversee these funds, and these metrics are how we hold ourselves to account." Even as this person made the point, she agreed that the current system was not working. For the foundation to track their metrics, they had to get data from grantees, and that created more work for all involved. While the intention may have been accountability, it was not clear that the result was accountability.

In this new era, philanthropy must reimagine learning in ways that deepens our understanding of how social change happens. Jara Dean-Coffey, CEO of jdcPARTNERSHIPS and founder of Equitable Evaluation Initiative, shares: "Learning is an integral organizational capacity, not an isolated function or role. It is part of being strategic and should be held as the responsibility of all and weaved in as a regular and routine practice."[4]

Jara introduced the Equitable Evaluation Framework (EEF) to reflect the values and intentions that drive foundations and nonprofits with twenty-first-century definitions of objectivity, validity, rigor, and embracing complexity.[5] The framework is grounded in the practice of continual learning, with all engaged in recognizing how culture, context, history, and power shape evaluative work. Jara notes:

> The predominant approach to evaluation comes from a different time and a very specific set of circumstances. It is laden with implicit beliefs about what it is, who should do it, how it

should be done, and what (and whose) purpose it should serve. The Equitable Evaluation Framework is a response to these disconnects and an invitation to philanthropy to revisit and refine the core concepts that inform evaluation and learning efforts and fundamentally evolve how we know what we know.[6]

Real Accountability Flows Two Ways

If evaluation metrics and strategic plans are in charge, who is accountable?

Like much in our sector, there is very little that philanthropy is legally required to do when it comes to funding strategies and how we are accountable to those strategies. In the absence of regulations and other legal forms of accountability, many of us create processes—strategies and metrics—in an effort to be perceived as accountable. And yet, these efforts don't make for true accountability.

How might we locate accountability within our relationships with grantees and measure how deeply we listen, how responsive we are to their needs, and how we show up in partnership? What are the avenues for creating cultural and process-oriented mechanisms of accountability? Would it be learning from our steps and missteps and sharing and applying those lessons? Would it be building clarity about what matters to us, and sharing that transparently in our relationships with our nonprofit partners?

We have tied our own hands, but we can also remove the knot—by learning to trust the people who are charged with getting money out the door. By learning as a sector how to be strategic, not in the way we've been taught is the norm, but by clarifying our values, deepening our relationships, and learning how to be responsive to complexity and emergent community needs.

PRACTICE PROMPTS

Looking Back: Seeing the Artifacts

Materials

Provide large sheets of paper, markers, sticky notes, and a laptop.

Activity

1. Divide your team into small groups of three to five people. Each group is a *New York Times* Styles Desk team, twenty years from now.

2. The task is to draft a short article about revisiting philanthropy's approaches to strategy and evaluation today.

3. Each team will present their articles at a "press conference" and take questions.

4. Give bonus points to teams that imagine and reference how these practices have evolved.

Looking Ahead: New Era Strategy and Evaluation

Materials

Provide large sheets of paper, markers, sticky notes, and a timer.

Activity

1. Divide participants into teams of three to five people.

2. Each team brainstorms a future philanthropic approach to strategy and evaluation, which they will share back with visual representations (a poster or storyboard) and creative presentations (skits, prototypes, infographics).

3. Include steps to take today to work toward these future norms.

4. Teams present their future philanthropy approaches in a pitch-session format.

5. Facilitate a group discussion on common themes and actionable next steps.

Reflection: On Learning

What are you trying to learn about as you fund, and how do you share that learning with the field? Can you assess how much you and your team are listening to and learning from grantees?

Fund Complexity and Wholeness

We live in a time of intersecting crises, and yet, much of philanthropy is designed to solve challenges as if they were separate and distinct. This chapter explores what becomes possible in this new era when our funding is designed for complexity and wholeness.

I met labor leader Andrea Dehlendorf, a cofounder and executive director of United for Respect (UFR) early in my tenure at GSF. Andrea and her coworker were looking to raise funds for the "Respect the Bump" campaign to protect the rights of pregnant Walmart workers.[1]

UFR members included pregnant Walmart workers who had their requests for workplace accommodations to limit exposure to toxic chemicals and reduce heavy lifting denied. These workers began organizing other pregnant Walmart workers from across the country, initially demanding workplace accommodations and paid family leave. Walmart is the single largest employer in the United States, with over two million employees worldwide.[2] Their policies not only impact their direct employees but influence the norms of other employers.

As I listened to Andrea and her coworker share their stories and their plans, I could hear how these workers and their organizing would change the world. It was also obvious to me that United for Respect was a fit for two of GSF's core program areas: reproductive *and* economic justice. I left our meeting excited at the prospect of GSF supporting such a powerful movement partner.

But that didn't happen. At least not for a long while. After the trip, I shared what I'd learned with the program officers leading the two portfolios. In my enthusiasm, I mentioned that supporting this group seemed like "doubly a good fit." When they declined to fund United for Respect despite a clear alignment with our work, values, and goals, I was genuinely confused.

It turned out my excitement about the work being doubly a good fit had translated to "not a fit at all" in the existing organizational structure. Both program officers took the fact that this work was a good fit beyond, not just in, their portfolio to mean that it must be on the margins of their work. Essentially, they were asking, Why should I fund it when someone else could?

This is a typical grantee-funder story in many ways. The moral for nonprofits and movements is: If you want to get funding, fit neatly and singularly into one narrowly crafted funding priority. Caroline Picker, a development director with Organized Power in Numbers, describes how this plays out at her organization. Member-driven with a base that is majority women of color, Organized Power in Numbers has struggled to tap new sources of funding for their housing justice and climate workforce development work because they are pigeonholed into worker-power funding portfolios.

Caroline shared that a program officer advised her, "Be careful how much you talk about certain aspects or locations of your work, because it may shift how we think about you as an organization, which could hurt your overall chances to get funding because we have very well-defined buckets that you may no longer clearly fit into."[3] The organization feels they need to "tiptoe around how we honestly and accurately reflect our work and what we are excited about because of how the lines are drawn." Caroline helped me understand that it isn't just portfolios that are siloed, but relationships too. "Because of the way that pots of money are organized, funders often don't have strong relationships beyond their issue-area silos that they can leverage to help grantees access new sources of funding."[4]

The idea that funding priorities should be narrow is a philanthropic default that is baked into strategies across the spectrum, from large foundations to modest individual donors. The strategic philanthropy movement has hammered this point, that effective philanthropy is rooted in "narrowly and specifically" defined priorities. The status quo of philanthropic practice has foundations and donors spending inordinate amounts of time trying to perfect their strategies, getting narrower and narrower in focus, while outside foundation doors, the world is on fire and grantseekers are increasingly shaping their work for the complexity at the heart of these times.

The influential philanthropy-advising field tends to share the perspective that narrowly crafted funding priorities are a prerequisite for effective philanthropy. For example, Rockefeller Philanthropy Advisors, in their publication "Your Philanthropy Roadmap," shares with donors:

> Once you've identified the area(s) of concentration for your philanthropy, you'll probably have to narrow your focus. Broad fields like education and the environment are convenient categories, but are obviously too big for any donor to tackle. You'll want to look at the components of those fields—early learning; primary and secondary school; higher education. Even within those areas you'll probably need to move to a more specific focus—perhaps by topic within the area (teacher training for primary/secondary school), by region, or by type of educational institution.[5]

While this advice may seem sound, it creates unseen barriers for groundbreaking organizations like United for Respect, Organized Power in Numbers, and so many others who are working in contexts that are complex and cut across issues, topics, and regions. The risk of funders having a narrow focus is that complex, intersectional, and impactful work will fall outside the narrow category.

When donors craft narrow boxes that grantees must fit into, what is revealed is only a tiny slice of the bigger picture. Organizations do their work in the messiness of the real world, where issues are interconnected and always evolving. When we ask grantee partners to contort and compartmentalize to get funding through our own lens, we miss opportunities to see beyond our imposed boundaries, where the most powerful, intersectional work often happens.

In our dynamic times of intersecting crises, there is a fundamental mismatch between philanthropy's propensity to contract and narrow and nonprofits' need to remain open and agile to meet their communities' goals. What results is a wider gap between funder-driven strategy and reality. The more relevant approach for these times is to create funding categories that are expansively conceived, to hold the complexity and intersectionality of community lives and needs, and to do so with an ethic of solidarity.

"Not My Issue" Will Be Our Downfall

In 2008 I was hired to lead the development of a new donor collaborative, the RISE Together Fund, to support organizations challenging post-9/11 Islamophobia. The two large foundations who initially launched the fund had program areas focused on human rights and national security. As a South Asian who had worked in the community, I understood Islamophobia as a racial justice issue and a threat to our democracy.

As a collaborative fund, we were both a grantmaker and a grantseeker. In my role raising resources, I would meet with prospective donors, whose values I shared, to invite them to support this crosscutting and impactful work. A racial justice program officer would suggest that I speak with the immigration funders, and the immigration funders suggested that I talk to the democracy funders. In meeting after meeting, they listened to me explain the work, and then apologetically responded, "It's really great work, Dimple. It just doesn't fit into my portfolio."

Meanwhile, beyond philanthropy, conservatives were engaged in efforts to spread Islamophobia. Between 2010 and 2016, anti-Muslim activists introduced 194 bills in 39 state legislatures across the country to ban Sharia law from being considered in US courts.[6] A ballot measure in

Kansas banning Sharia law passed by 70 percent.[7] The far right was testing whether a drummed-up fear of Muslims could motivate the right, much like attacks on same-sex marriage in past years, and anti-trans bills today, and in Kansas, they found their answer. In 2015 then-candidate Donald Trump announced that were he to become President, he would institute a "total and complete shutdown" of the country's borders to Muslims.

The broader donor community had an opportunity to support a safer future for all of us, but had declined to act, unable to see past the "program area" they'd created. They saw this as an issue narrowly related to Islamophobia rather than as a threat to pluralism and democracy itself. They underestimated how tied our fates are. They were program-aligned but worldview-agnostic.

Many of us working in philanthropy recognize that we are in a moment when our democracy is under extreme threat. In 2023, more than 589 bills targeting the health and safety of trans kids and adults were introduced.[8] The push to ban "critical race theory" has taken hold in states where people want to erase rather than acknowledge this country's racist history and its ongoing impacts. Political retaliation has become commonplace, as we saw when two Tennessee lawmakers were expelled from the state legislature for protesting against gun violence in the aftermath of a school shooting.[9] Conservative funders have worked in coordinated ways to move dollars and attention from one "issue" to the next, understanding this is all part of the same fight.

Will the broader community of donors and foundations understand the magnitude of these times, and embrace a more expansive approach to funding that centers the work as it is experienced in communities? Or will they look back and say:

> "We couldn't fight critical race theory because we didn't have an un-ban books program area."

> "We cared about kids being safe at school, getting gender-affirming care, and surviving, but the foundation didn't have a healthy trans kids portfolio."

> "We would have loved to support (urgent issue of the day), but our hands were tied with (perceived time, geographic, or issue area constraint)."

It is especially important to uplift the long-term movement, power-building, and other on-the-ground work led by organizers in communities that rarely fall neatly into funding priorities because it is by definition and design inter-sectional. Community wisdom and lived experience tell us that issues are never singular, and that power cannot be siloed.

Values as Strategy

Going back to Andrea and the Walmart organizers, I'm happy to share that United for Respect was one of the first grants under the foundation's new direction. How did we get there? First, our board and staff had to identify what we were trying to achieve—not from the confines of individual pro-gram areas but based on our clarified deepest-held values. We also sought community input, asking our grantees how *they* describe their work when talking to their friends, family, community members—and not to funders. Across all our separate siloed programs we heard one answer repeatedly: power-building.

Our values, now clear, became the basis of our grantmaking strategy. A few months later, we did away with separate program areas and moved all our grantmaking into an intersectional and collaborative portfolio: Build-ing Voice and Power. Our grantees had given us the road map to make this change.

While we were working internally to align ourselves, United for Respect had been busy successfully organizing for workplace accommodations and winning paid family leave for Walmart employees.[10] Their work and vision led them to getting the largest retail employer to offer something even the federal government doesn't offer. These are the kinds of groups funders often miss because their work spans beyond and across narrow areas. *We* almost missed the opportunity to support their incredible work.

Showing Up Fully

As we were preparing to move into our broader power-building portfolio, I called longtime grantee partner LA Black Worker Center and spoke to Lola Smallwood Cuevas, the executive director, to get her feedback on the shift.

I asked Lola, "When we fund you next, it will be as part of our Building Voice and Power program rather than an Economic Justice program. We expect the grant to stay the same but are happy to hear any concerns or questions you might have about this shift and how it might impact your program."

Lola's response stopped me in my tracks. "Wow," she said, pausing. "I feel like that would allow me to show up whole, and for us to show you who we really are, and the wholeness of our work. Not just the part about economic justice, not just the part that speaks to your funding area." I hadn't expected a longtime grantee partner with whom we had a strong relationship, who I thought we invited to show up fully, to have something they felt they had to hold back.

I asked her to say more. Lola shared, "We've actually been leading work for a while now around climate, connecting our unemployed members with the new climate economy. This has meant a lot to the community we serve, but it's climate-related, so we haven't shared that work with you." There was something so powerful in hearing Lola describe what it would mean for her to no longer have to compartmentalize her work, the needs of the community, and what she could share with me, in order to get funding. She could, as she said, show up fully.

Showing Up Whole

Audre Lorde famously noted that people don't lead "single-issue lives."[11] Yet too many funders continue to fund as if they did. In the process, they hold back progress and miss key opportunities for protection and transformation. Legal scholar and law professor Kimberlé Crenshaw coined the term "intersectionality" two decades ago and more recently explained, "Intersectionality is a lens through which you can see where power comes and collides, where it interlocks and intersects. It's not simply that there's a race problem here, a gender problem here, and a class or LBGTQ problem there. Many times that framework erases what happens to people who are subject to all of these things."[12] Intersectionality means understanding one another's fullness, not just our parts. Linda Sarsour, a Palestinian Muslim American activist who has long fought for reproductive rights, immigrant rights, and police reform, talks about the limitations of philanthropy's narrowly defined funding areas—not just on the work, but on organizers. Despite her cross-cutting advocacy, until recently she has only ever received funding from national security–focused funders. "I'm so ready to show up and be whole in my work," Linda shared with me on a panel years ago.

In this new era, we can practice philanthropic solidarity, which is an invitation to see a more just future as one in which we understand the intersections between issues.

> What if, when they came for our trans sisters, reproductive justice funders stepped up, understanding the dangers to all of us when political leaders coordinate attacks on bodily autonomy?

> What if, in their climate justice solutions, environmental funders recognized the need to center Disability Justice and ensure that cleaner, safer futures were being built for all, not just some?

> What if all funders recognized the role anti-Black racism plays in our society and invested in telling real stories about our country's painful history, putting an end to "critical race theory" bans and other attempts to divide us?

In this new era, we need to support our grantee partners and community leaders in ways that allow them to show up and be whole in their work. When philanthropy remains bound by silos, funders miss operating from a place of connection and become easily divided by opponents. It is our most deeply held values—not our narrowest strategies—that will help guide us to the future that communities seek and deserve.

PRACTICE PROMPTS

Ask Your Grantee, Ask Your Funder

For funders: "How do you describe your work when you are talking with your family and your community? How does that shift when you are talking to funders?" Listen for what is missing.

For nonprofits: "How do you describe our work when you are talking with your colleagues or peer funders? What's the narrowest and broadest way you view it?" Listen for what is missing.

Beyond the Gaps Funding Forum

Materials: large sheets of paper, sticky notes, markers

1. Ask participants to write issues of the day that are of concern to communities and grantseekers and relevant to your mission, but fall outside of a funding portfolio, on sticky notes.

2. Participants place their sticky notes on a large sheet of paper or board titled "Not My Issue."

3. Look over the collective list and identify similarities and themes. What is the cumulative effect of these issues struggling to get funding?

4. Brainstorm a list of ideas for how funders can support emergent challenges and other mission-relevant work that falls outside funding silos.

PRACTICE

9

See Opportunity in Every Crisis

Crisis is a feature of our times. How philanthropy responds in these moments and beyond them is more critical than ever. This chapter provides crisis operating instructions for how funders can not only rise to the occasion but use each crisis to affirmatively build toward a more just, resilient, and sustainable future.

"Mama, why is it still dark out?"

It was around 11 a.m., on September 9, 2020, and the sky was dark with an eerie orange glow. For those living in the Bay Area, this day came to be known as the "Orange Day." The sun never quite came out, blocked by a sky full of smoke coming from raging wildfires.

I remember feeling a visceral dread in my body. It wasn't just the fires and the dark sky. We were six months into a global pandemic, following a summer of racial justice reckoning, and now you could taste the wildfire smoke in the air and feel its burn in your eyes. Crisis upon crisis upon crisis, all at the same time. You likely have your own Orange Day, a time when the climate crisis came into clearer focus and closer to home.

The term *polycrisis* has been gaining in popularity since it was featured in the World Economic Forum's 2023 *Global Risks Report* to describe the converging crises that "shape a unique, uncertain, and turbulent decade to come."[1] Polycrisis captures how—together—these crises have compounding effects, such that "the overall impact far exceeds the sum of each part."[2] Whatever funders may be planning to support in the coming years, it will no doubt be shaped by the polycrisis unfolding: rising authoritarianism, climate emergency, financial collapse, the many manifestations of rising inequality, and war and violence. In this new era of philanthropy, we must be ready with polysolutions, things we can do that will create rapid, profound, and lasting change.

Too often when a crisis occurs, the go-to playbook for funding is disaster philanthropy, characterized by short-term, one-time funding focused on immediate relief. It's what we usually see after a hurricane, landslide, fire, or other natural disaster. A Candid survey documented the disaster funding cliff, finding that COVID-related funding declined by 31 percent from 2020 to 2021.[3] While disaster philanthropy may have the right instinct—to move resources and move them quickly—the time-limited, fragmented, short-term nature of it can leave communities no better prepared for future events, and sometimes even worse off.

From Crisis to Transformation

Author and activist Naomi Klein writes about how opportunity accompanies crisis, with "a long and proud history of crises sparking progressive transformation on a societal scale."[4] Too often, moments of crisis have been seized to enact harmful, fear-based policies that benefit the few. But Klein reminds us, "Moments of great crisis and peril do not need to knock us backward: They can also catapult us forward.... To win in a moment of true crisis, we also need a bold and forward-looking yes: a plan for how to rebuild and respond to the underlying causes."[5]

In the aftermath of the murder of George Floyd by police, funders responded in a number of usual ways—with grants, task forces, and statements. Communities were rising up for racial justice in historic numbers, many still reeling from the ongoing pandemic and with deep concerns about the fast-approaching election. There was a palpable hunger for a deeper response.

Crystal Hayling, an experienced leader in philanthropy and then-executive director of the Libra Foundation, understood that this moment of crisis was an opportunity for transformative change. She was determined that philanthropy's response would be different, deeper, and longer-lasting. That summer, Crystal launched the Democracy Frontlines Fund (DFF) to support Black-led racial justice organizing, recruiting a set of twelve funding partners, many of whom were committing to this work for the first time at this scale.

DFF is unique in its design. The fund engaged its funding partners as participants on a years-long racial justice learning journey. Grantees were vetted by an advisory Brain Trust—women of color leaders who bring decades of experience in social and racial justice movements, and with deep ties to communities. Grants were made with as few obstacles as possible and went out in the form of multiyear, flexible general operating support—multimillion-dollar gifts to a slate of national Black-led organizations building power and working on issues of community safety, free and fair elections, climate, food, and land justice.

The fund intentionally approaches democracy "from the perspective of those most systematically excluded from it, many of whom have fought most vehemently to secure it," according to Hayling. It aims "to deepen philanthropy's understanding of what democracy means—that it's not just about walking into a voting booth. We are engaging communities in a learning process because we have not necessarily been great at understanding all the facets of practicing democracy."[6]

For the funding partners, the learning journey cultivated strong relationships, and for many, transformation. Daniel Lau, DFF's initiative officer, noted the importance of spaces to reflect, "because so much of the change we need to see is also within us and our institutions."[7] These conversations, he notes, are not always comfortable. The DFF funder community wades into deep waters with funding partners about movement and organizing campaigns like defunding the police for more community-based public safety strategies. Throughout, DFF remains committed not to funder and donor comfort but to transformational change. As Daniel noted, "You have to have a certain level of discomfort to experience change."[8]

A crisis changes us, rarely leaving us in the place where we began. Funders are positioned to shape moments of crisis into times that move us toward greater interdependence and justice, times that are defined by additional resources, support, and care. As we saw with the racial justice uprisings, the COVID-19 pandemic, the wildfires, and democracy under attack—funders have the opportunity to step into action, loosen rigid requirements, ask grantees what they need, and help build a runway to something new.

As we enter a new era of philanthropy, we must develop practices that meet moments of crisis with clear visions of the future that communities seek to build and with resourcing tools that are more expansive and durable than disaster philanthropy.

The Beginning of a List of Crisis Operating Instructions

I say "beginning" because I expect that in the coming years, we will continue to learn and collectively add to this list.

1. **Start with a power analysis.** Crises hold a mirror up to us and show us who has power and who we are systematically leaving behind. When a crisis hits, ask: Who is most impacted? Fund in a way that recognizes the disproportionate impacts on those most marginalized.

2. **Look at causes, not just effects.** Crises sometimes come with a narrative of inevitability: "natural" disasters. Nature can be a terrifying force, but the worst impacts are almost always human-made. This is true for hurricanes like Katrina, pandemics like COVID-19, and economic crises.

3. **Be willing to fund things that don't fit into your pre-crisis funding areas.** What is most needed in a given moment may not necessarily be what is described in your funding areas. Listen to community and grantee partners who understand how crises are impacting them, and what they need, in real time.

4. **Open the door to change.** Crises create openings for radical change, because during a crisis, norms shift quickly. As a funder, what are the ideas and dreams that can now go from the margin to the center with your support? Your crisis funding can also be transformational and build a more just and sustainable future.

5. **Don't let the government off the hook.** When there are gaps in public funding, it can be tempting to fill them, but funders must be careful not to take the place of government. Remember you weren't elected by anyone! Instead, how can you fund organizations that can hold the government accountable and advocate for their communities' needs?

6. **Check in on your people.** Funders: ask your grantees, simply, what they need—as humans, as social change agents, as those caring for communities. Center people: Crisis is also when we build with each other. Move with care for your staff and for your grantee's staff.

7. **Avoid crisis fatigue.** Take the time to slow down and feel your feelings, ground in your body, and take affirmative steps to mitigate overwhelm. The multiplicity and frequency of crises does not mean that each crisis deserves a lesser response. Staying present and grounded amid crisis is essential for funders seeking to meet the moment.

8. **Have a flexible and responsive spending policy.** Have a system in place for rapidly adjusting your foundation's spending decision if needed, so that when crises occur, you can quickly access new funds and get them out the door.

9. **Leave better infrastructure.** In every crisis, have a goal of leaving behind a strengthened infrastructure. With each crisis, be willing to fund the changed conditions and the new possibilities with multiyear long-term support.

10. **Don't assume your experience is everyone's experience.** Listen to grantee partners and community members who are living through the same time but may be navigating different circumstances. If you measure a crisis based on your experience, you will almost certainly get it wrong.

PRACTICE PROMPTS

Be the Polysolution to Today's Polycrisis: Scenario Planning

1. Make a set of cards with an individual crisis on each card using the World Economic Forum's *Global Risks Report 2023* "Global Risks Landscape: An Interconnections Map," on page 10.[9]

2. Someone in the group selects two cards and, as a group, you discuss the implications on your giving in the event of these two concurrent crises. What opportunities might exist during these crises?

3. Now add in two more cards. How does the picture change? What opportunities exist from here?

4. Toward polysolutions: What can you put in place today that will help you be ready to fund both the crises and the opportunities of the future? Which crisis operating instructions will help build capacity for the moments ahead?

All Together Now

Modern philanthropy is both imagined and structured as an individual enterprise, with donors and foundations conceiving of and working toward their missions on their own. Funders who are students of social change understand that social transformation comes from collective action. This chapter explores the transformations that become possible when we see ourselves as part of a bigger whole and forge ways to move together.

As a program officer, I would ask grantees, "Who do you partner with?" Their answers about the relationships they built, nurtured, and prioritized—and the depth of those connections—told me a lot about the organization's ability to achieve its goals. But this question was about more than just effectiveness. I was asking, "Who are your people?"

While this is a common question we ask grantee partners, rarely do we ask funders, Who are your people? What are you learning from them and alongside them? What are you creating and supporting together?

Today there are more than 120,000 foundations registered in the United States alone, and 130,000 foundations in Europe.[1] Many foundations work on solving problems the nature and scale of which guarantee they cannot be fixed by a single organization. While foundations may recognize themselves as belonging to a broader ecosystem, how they work is rarely designed for collective approaches. Rather, modern philanthropy takes as its starting point a donor exercising their individual preferences, often described as "donor freedom," for how they want to allocate their excess wealth. The gilded philanthropy narrative of "my money" gives rise to the current structural form of the private foundation: an institution designed based on a donor's intent and largely accountable to itself and its board. The design of the philanthropic field dubiously assumes progress will flow (fingers crossed) because of many different institutions, each on their own, identifying a problem and then funding its solution. As foundations carve out their respective lanes with unique mission statements, visions, and approaches, they rarely invite feedback, or pushback, from anyone outside their organization.

The image that comes to mind when I consider today's individualistic approach to philanthropy is one of those multi-person bicycles, except here, we are all biking in different directions, and so we end up just expending lots of energy essentially going nowhere.[2]

"What's wrong with differently pointed tandem bikes?" a donor might ask. Well, they don't work if you want to move forward, and in these high-stakes times it matters more than ever that we know where we're going and have the collective tools to get there.

We are in the midst of what economists call the Great Wealth Transfer, with an anticipated 18 trillion new dollars expected to flow into the charitable sector by 2048.[3] Do we really believe the best solution moving forward is for each donor to create their individual strategies and institutions? More than a hundred years of this choose-your-own-adventure approach to philanthropy has resulted in more funding and more philanthropies. However, there is little evidence that this structural form is designed for broader impact.

What if, instead of today's individualized approach to philanthropy, foundations saw their work as collective? What if our model was an ecosystem of shared purpose, vision, strategy, and an ability to be in deep relationship with one another? Where the collective nature of our work could be an expression of mutual accountability? Philanthropy, acting collectively, can not only fill resource gaps but also address the deeper structural challenges of how power is organized in our society.

This chapter invites us to practice a collective approach to resourcing a more just and sustainable future. From there, the door opens to everything collaboration offers—what we learn together, how we are changed in community, the sharpness of our strategies, our ability to make meaning, and a more powerful path to wide-scale change.

Funding Together

One way that funders are moving beyond atomized individual approaches is through collaborative funding. My first experience with this approach was in 2008 when I was hired to build the RISE Together Fund, a donor collaborative building an inclusive democracy by investing in grassroots leaders challenging Islamophobia. Leading a collaborative fund was simultaneously some of the most challenging, creative, and impactful work I've done in philanthropy.

At our best, the collaborative was able to fund bolder and more innovative efforts than any one partner could have on their own. As a collective, we understood risk differently than many of our partner funders. We partnered with grantees in the field and supported experiments in shared field infrastructure, like a communications hub that over one hundred grantees used to increase their capacity and alignment. Our relative distance from donors and their intent made it possible for us to be guided by grantee needs and shaped by grantee voice. We learned together, our shared insights rippling through each donor's institution, shaping foundation strategies well beyond our fund.

Vehicles for collaborative funding like giving circles and mutual aid have long existed. A recent Bridgespan Group report, commissioned by the Gates Foundation's Philanthropic Partnerships Team, finds that philanthropic collaboration is on the rise and experiencing a "new era of popularity and ambition." Interest and investment in collaborative giving has grown over the last decade as a result of both an increase in wealth and a growing interest in new ways of giving.[4]

"Rather than start a foundation, more young donors are participating in donor collaboratives, which allow people to give more quickly than if they had to set up and staff a foundation."[5] That's one of several takeaways outlined in the *Chronicle of Philanthropy*'s review of megadonors, anticipating future trends. As Nick Tedesco, CEO of the National Center for Family Philanthropy, observed:

> We're moving from an era that historically has centered the donor and the expertise of an institution to a place that centers the expertise of community. You can have leaner infrastructure that has a much more collaborative approach with community honoring their skills, their expertise.[6]

The "leanness meets specialists" argument for collaborative funding resonates with my own experience funding collaboratives. At GSF, we had a lean program team, and when our strategy evolved to include funding to state and locally based grassroots organizations, we needed more expertise and capacity. Collaborative funds like the Amplify Fund and the Partnership Fund offered us a way to invest in state and local work.[7] Staff at these funds understood the context, had deep relationships with community partners, and were able to fund a thoughtful ecosystem of organizations. Participating in these funds gave us the benefit of partnerships with likeminded funders as well as participation in communities of practice where we experimented with community-centric forms of funding. Giving up this focus on *our* needs, strategies, and preferences created a pathway for us to engage in grantmaking that aligned with the needs, strategies, and preferences of community members.

While I have seen the tremendous impact made possible by coming together, it is also true that at their worst, collective funding vehicles can move slowly, be held hostage by one donor partner, and waste the precious expertise of staff on constant fundraising. There is a myth that pooled funding is a cheaper way to fund, and stingy approaches to collaborative funding only dilute the potential for impact.

When it comes to collaborative funding, it is not the form or structure of funding that is inherently transformative. Rather it is the *stance* that collaborative funding represents: the humility that is inherent in saying, We can't do this on our own. And the muscles we develop as we find new, intentional ways to work together.

A More Democratic Philanthropy

Since modern philanthropy's origin, one of the most consistent critiques of it has been that it is antidemocratic, with decision-making concentrated in the hands of the most wealthy and powerful few. There is something radical, then, in how collaborative funding brings in those voices and perspectives, often not at the decision-making table. The structural innovations of collaborative and participatory funding create an opening for new types of governance, new types of leadership, and new types of culture—all steps toward democratizing philanthropy.

Collective giving, that is "individuals pooling their resources, knowledge, and networks together to support a cause collectively chosen by the group," is a "growing force in US philanthropy." A recent report by the Dorothy A. Johnson Center for Philanthropy, "In Abundance: An Analysis of the Thriving Landscape of Collective Giving in the U.S.," examines this growing landscape, with authors describing collective giving as "a form of philanthropy that draws upon the traditions of mutual aid and solidarity among marginalized communities, that by its very nature engenders connection . . . both within groups and between them, and celebrates generosity and elevates community-driven solutions." Giving circles in the US moved $3.1 billion in the last six years and mobilized 370,000 philanthropists.[8]

Philanthropy Together, an organization that supports a growing global movement of giving circles and donor collaboratives as part of their mission to diversify and democratize philanthropy, identified a connection between democracy and giving in a range of collective giving efforts from community-specific giving circles, like Black, Latinx, and Asian and Pacific Islander giving circles, to collaborative funds. They note an increased use by collaborative funds of participatory and democratic decision-making structures and also an increased propensity toward civic engagement for individuals who participate in collective giving.

"Collective giving creates a forum for the practice of the soft skills of democracy. Representational democracy is about an individual voice, but it only works if it's everybody's voice together. The shift we see with collective giving is a shift toward collective power," shared Isis Krause, Philanthropy Together's chief of strategy. Sara Lomelin, executive director of Philanthropy Together, sees collaborative giving as helping donors see themselves as "part of the same ecosystem trying to make change."[9] This process of seeing yourself as part of something bigger translates into belonging, purpose, and connection to community for donors engaged in collective giving.[10]

In this new era, donors are beginning to realize the power inherent in bringing in different perspectives. In 2024, Melinda French Gates announced a $1 billion commitment to advancing women's power globally through her organization Pivotal Ventures. A key component to her strategy is to move $20 million each to twelve global leaders so that each could direct these funds to work they deem is crucially helping to progress women's health and well-being. In a *New York Times* op-ed, Gates describes the diverse cohort she is entrusting with decision-making power:

> That group—which includes the former prime minister of New Zealand Jacinda Ardern, the athlete and maternal-health advocate Allyson Felix, and an Afghan champion of girls' education, Shabana Basij-Rasikh—represents a wide range of expertise and experience. I'm eager to see the landscape of funding opportunities through their eyes, and the results their approaches unlock.[11]

An Alternative to Traditional Philanthropy and the Birth of Something New

When Bridgespan researchers studied ninety-seven collaborative-funding organizations, they came away with a surprising conclusion: Collaborative-giving platforms "differ from traditional philanthropy" in "their priorities and the means by which they operate."[12]

Bridgespan asked funding collaboratives to identify their primary giving priorities and found that collaborative funds ranked racial equity as a top issue, with economic mobility and climate change following. In contrast, the twenty-five largest institutional foundations and family foundations do not reference racial justice or racial equity in their mission statements.[13] The funding approaches that collaboratives use also differ significantly from mainstream philanthropy, with roughly a third of funds seeking "systemic change through building fields and movements." The study found a significant number of funds that transferred decision-making power to nonprofit leaders and community groups on the receiving end of grant-making. By experimenting with participatory approaches that bring those who receive funding into the decision-making process, collaborative funds are reimagining how power works in philanthropy.

In a sector that has long struggled to diversify at the leadership level, Bridgespan found that one-half of collaborative funds are led by people of color. This is in stark contrast to the 10 percent of US private foundations that are led by people of color. With this diversity comes a proximity to impacted communities and a range of perspectives that are missing in institutional philanthropy more broadly. The Bridgespan data highlighting diversity, power-sharing in decision making, and the centering of racial equity in collaborative giving suggests that when funders come together, they can practice a wholly different kind of philanthropy that is more aligned to the times. Jennifer Stout, deputy director of philanthropic partnerships at the Gates Foundation, describes collaborative funds as the future of equity-oriented philanthropy, "because of their greater focus on more distributed decision-making models, more proximate funding, and more trust-based funding."[14]

I asked Bridgit Antoinette Evans, CEO of the Pop Culture Collaborative, if she agreed with this assessment that by coming together, funders could transform philanthropic norms that hold us back from achieving greater progress. Her response offered both an important vision and clarity on what it will take for this vision to be realized:

> The brightest, best vision I could have for these [collaborative] funds is if they were intentionally designed to be a stage in a process of transferring power, redistributing wealth, and

creating more accountable philanthropic models. If that was the trajectory, then I think that the deep investment in funds led by and accountable to those communities—BIPOC communities, queer, transgender, expansive communities, disabled, immigrant, Muslim, and others that have been on the frontlines of aggression for so many generations—with the intention to genuinely repatriate and rematriate power and wealth, will set up a very powerful next stage. From there, we can open up the possibilities for a reinvention of the concept of philanthropy, maybe even the death of what we think of as philanthropy and the birth of something new.[15]

Bridgit's insight goes to the heart of what can shift when we come together: power, accountability, and even the meaning of grantmaking—from distributing grants to the redistribution of wealth.

Trust-Based Philanthropy Project: Evolving Philanthropic Practice Together

Months before the COVID-19 pandemic hit and foundations transformed many of their practices seemingly overnight, a group of funders, led by Whitman Institute, Headwaters Foundation, and Robert Sterling Clark Foundation, launched the Trust-Based Philanthropy (TBP) Project. In the years leading up to this launch, Pia Infante, former co-executive director at Whitman Institute, had assembled a diverse set of peers practicing philanthropy from a relational and power-aware stance to invite our strategic input on how we might scale these new approaches. The TBP Project was established with a mission to be a resource to foundations interested in changing their practice and leadership to become more trust-based and equity-centered.

When the project first started, it had a relatively modest following—predominantly funders from the Bay Area and New York, where some of the founding funders were based. In the months following the start of the pandemic, that following quickly grew, with upward of a thousand funders from around the United States and abroad registering for the project's offerings. Trust-based philanthropy found its audience in a time of crisis, as many funders realized that the gilded approaches to philanthropy were no longer working.

Shaady Salehi, executive director of the TBP Project, understood that transforming philanthropic practice was best done in community. She realized that to evolve their practices, funders needed to have a safe and real-time space to ask questions that they may not be able to ask inside their own institutions. The TBP Project launched an email list, the Trust-Based Peer Exchange, which grew to have more than a thousand practitioners as more and more people attended webinars. Daily, funders shared questions, and others replied with answers: Has anyone updated a grants contract to be trust-based? How have you reimagined the job description of a program officer? Does anyone have experience streamlining a grants management system? Grant contracts were shared and improved on, grants managers who had spent months researching platforms saved their colleagues the effort, and key foundation roles, titles, and functions were reimagined in real time. This cross-fertilization, facilitated by the TBP Project, accelerated the pace of change and transformed collective norms in the sector.

We need more spaces for funders to learn together, and out loud. Reflecting on how funders have evolved, Shaady shared:

> A major part of our organizing effort has relied on funders who are willing to be vulnerable enough to share the lessons they have learned in their work. This has inspired a sense of openness and curiosity among our network, one wherein lessons and challenges are seen as opportunities to learn and grow together.[16]

Grantees Benefit When We Find Ways to Work Together

In philanthropic cultures where the incentives all point to leading, sometimes what makes collective work possible is a willingness to follow.

In the days after the 2016 election, a group of peer foundation CEOs came together quickly and informally to strategize. We understood that frontline organizations were about to have dramatically increased needs, and we planned to go to our boards to ask for an increased payout. A few of us got quick approvals from our boards and now had additional rapid-response dollars to put out into the field. We soon realized, however, that if the fourteen of us were successful in getting funds for rapid-response work, grantees would now have the additional work and burden of applying to all fourteen of our foundations.

We began conversations about what collaboration might look like. Could we share an application? Could we share reports? While there was interest in the topic, it was also a busy and urgent time, and none of us had the bandwidth to launch a new collaborative fund.

One of my fellow CEOs, Nat Chioke Williams, emailed me to say that he and his board were feeling impatient and just wanted to do something. He attached a press release and said, we are going to send out a rapid-response request for proposals (RFP). I read over his RFP, and as it was drafted, it didn't sound like "us"—meaning that it was not written in the institutional voice of the organization I was leading. In substance, though, the work was exactly what we wanted to support with our additional rapid-response funding.

I picked up the phone, called Nat, and asked, "Can we do this with you?" I said, "We won't change the RFP, but rather you can just add our name, and double the pot of funds, and that way organizations don't need to apply to us both."

Holding the grantee impact with more weight than our organization's voice or process allowed us to become a collaborative effort we called the Defending the Dream Fund. By modeling coming together, Nat and I were able to bring others in too. Eventually, the partnership grew to include nine additional funders, and together we resourced critical work to defend frontline communities facing attacks.

A Common App for a Common Cause

In 1975, colleges and universities came together to streamline the college application process by creating a common application for students. In 2016, our newly formed Defending the Dream Fund team was wondering how to streamline our rapid response funding, and whether funders could share a common application.

This question grew into an exploration with Iara Peng, who had also been wondering whether there was a way for grantee applications also to be viewed by multiple funders. When we reached out to her, she was in the early stages of building JustFund, a nonprofit grantmaking portal designed to connect grantmakers and organizations. Our rapid response fund, Defending the Dream, became JustFund's first client for what became the first common grant application portal in the United States.

Our goal in working with JustFund was to have grantees apply for funding in a portal where their applications could be viewed by a broad community of funders looking to support similar work. Thanks to Just-Fund, our goal was realized, and organizations that applied for our funding went on to get funded by other foundations on the JustFund site. One of the first grantees to apply to Defending the Dream on this portal was the Native Organizers Alliance. Seven years later, Iara told me that their application was seen by other donors, and they raised an additional $470,000 on the JustFund platform. Iara shared:

> Philanthropy has been exclusionary for too long, so we have to change the way we give. When you create systems that ensure money moves to people closest to the solutions, our communities win. And with more efficient grantmaking processes, we can knock down the barriers and bottlenecks, letting the funds flow like a dam breaking and the water getting to the communities that are the driest.[17]

Today, the JustFund portal is used by 172 funds and foundations and has distributed over $297 million. Iara shared that grantees who applied for funding on JustFund have collectively saved thirty-eight years of time by using the common grant application.

We learned together. We moved together. So many ripples that came from this one question, "Can we do this together?"

Making Meaning and Taking Action Together

"If we're going to survive this current political moment, we need to continue prioritizing space for relationship-building and grounding ourselves in our shared aspirations for a more just future." Jonathan Jayes-Green, a board member of Hispanics in Philanthropy, shared this reflection on social media along with a photo—a group of joyful faces—taken at a gathering of Hispanics in Philanthropy and Native Americans in Philanthropy.

Community can be a site for transformation. I suspect that one reason that many leaders of color adopt approaches to philanthropy that are more rooted in community is that many of us build and belong to multiple communities where we are making meaning together. Our philanthropic practice draws on wisdom from the communities we belong to, which include people who are directly impacted by injustice.

I have been so grateful for the communities in philanthropy that I belong to where I've had space to imagine beyond the norms, learn from peers, and develop a standard for my work that surpassed and was distinct from what my board held me to. In my early years at GSF, our team was part of a small informal lunch club, self-named the How Club. We would gather with this group of five to eight colleagues and share with each other our experiments and curiosities around the impact flowing from the "how" of our philanthropy.

In this space, How Club members shared what we were learning as we streamlined grantmaking processes, increased grant terms, and invested in sabbatical programs. So many of us from this small lunch club, including Pia Infante and John Esterle from the Whitman Institute, Carrie Avery from the Durfee Foundation, and Holly Bartling and me from GSF, went on to be active strategists of the Trust-Based Philanthropy Project, where we brought our learnings and inquiries to a sector-wide platform. Seeds planted in this small learning community grew into a movement that has transformed a set of philanthropic norms.

In 2020, I was grateful to three trusted CEO colleagues who brought together a group of foundation CEOs to build a community of "antiracist CEOs." In this confidential space, we made meaning together about what we could do in our roles, and what our grantees needed from our organizations. We also shared resources and lessons on shaping racial-equity philanthropic strategies. It was so important to have a space where we could collectively figure out the boldest thing we can do to advance racial equity in our roles as private foundation CEOs. There are incredible resources that exist about how to take your organization through a racial equity journey, but nothing takes the place of being in a community where you can share and grapple with how truly challenging it is to take organizations of wealth and privilege and transform them into vehicles for freedom.

The good news is that the philanthropic ecosystem has a set of organizations that are well-suited for serving as these meaning-making, action-taking hubs. Some are geographically oriented regional grantmaker associations; others are oriented by subject matter. Some, like the National Center for Family Philanthropy, offer important spaces for trustees to find each other and to learn and advance their practice together. In recent years many of these organizations have become more intentional about creating community and opportunities for cross-organizational learning and transformation that positions the philanthropic sector to better address shared challenges.

When we shift our philanthropy toward a collective approach, we are moving away from gilded philanthropy, shifting our story of scarcity, and beginning to embody the abundance of resources that exists in the sector. In this new era of philanthropy, we are beginning to understand ourselves as belonging to a bigger ecosystem. That belonging shifts our understanding of what we can accomplish together. Sara and Isis at Philanthropy Together describe a giving circle member who couldn't imagine the impact they might have with their own giving capacity, but when those resources are combined with twenty, fifty, or a hundred others who share their goals and values, they saw the power in the collective.[18] I've seen a similar reality among institutional donors whose dreams for justice are limited by the size of their grant budgets, but when working collaboratively, their investment and impact are multiplied.

Moving money together can be transformative. And developing collective philanthropic practices is bigger than just moving money together. It encompasses the many ways that we can make meaning and take action together. We move from an individual-centered philanthropy to a collective one by engaging in, belonging to, and creating shared communities in which we can go beyond the norms and narratives of our institutions. There is a power that is unlocked when we belong to communities where there is enough trust for us to grapple together, imagine new ways, and even sometimes change our minds.

The invitation here is that we come out from behind our desks, venture beyond our institutions, and find one another. Let's truly engage one another on what is needed in this time, what we are learning, and how we can invest as an ecosystem in a more just and sustainable future.

PRACTICE PROMPTS

Learning from Failure Together

Host a *Moth*-style storytelling session at a conference, inviting peers to share their worst philanthropy stories. These can be grantseeker stories (we need more of these!) or funder stories, with the goal of sharing the failures in a fun and collaborative setting so that we can learn together.

Find Your People

Audit the collective spaces you are in to make sure these are communities where you are evolving with others and have opportunities to share, reflect on, and change your beliefs and behaviors.

Rethinking Leadership

Revisit how your organization evaluates team members to ensure that collaboration is valued and incentivized. How might your organization's understanding of leadership need to evolve to make room for more collective work?

Epilogue

Another world is not only possible, she is on her way.
On a quiet day, I can hear her breathing.

—ARUNDHATI ROY, *War Talk*

When you imagine a future that is more just and sustainable, in which all our descendants are flourishing, do you see philanthropy as we know it today? I find it hard to imagine the philanthropy we know today existing in that future.

In a more democratic and healthier society, I imagine resources for the public good will be held and governed over in public forms. Extreme inequality won't exist as it does today, and people will have a greater voice in the decisions that shape their lives.

I do imagine that the core meaning of philanthropy, love of humanity, will be alive and thriving. It will infuse our structures, systems, and culture. The love of humanity will be expressed in countless ways in societies that have been structured to take care of each other and the planet.

Philanthropic forms that were imagined as existing in perpetuity will come to be understood as transitional. The alchemy and practices of moving resources and power will transform resources into a more just and sustainable future. The highest purposes of private philanthropy will be achieved, and the form will no longer be necessary.

My friend and colleague Regan Pritzker, a trustee of Kataly Foundation and the Libra Foundation, describes her work as a donor as "hospicing philanthropy." She uses the word *hospice* because it speaks to the caring required in times of transition. The call to hospice philanthropy as we knew it reminds us that all transitions come with loss. We can meet this moment of transition in philanthropy with care and compassion, and a willingness to let go.

In this future I imagine, this book has become an artifact. Years from now, this book may be picked up as a reminder of a pivotal time, when philanthropy was evolving—finally—to meet the moment and support the broader transitions underway. The alchemy we practiced brought us to this. What will that future look like? That's up to all of us.

I believe it's a future where resources are distributed, not hoarded;

Where the economy works for all people, not the few;

Where we live in a democracy that is fair and functional and felt;

Where people have a voice in the decisions that shape their lives;

Where we live in balance with our resources.

A world where today's philanthropy is an artifact, a symbol of a time we left behind.

NOTES

Introduction

1. Philanthropy Roundtable, "Statistics on U.S. Generosity," November 20, 2023, *https://www.philanthropyroundtable.org/almanac/statistics-on-u-s-generosity/*; Cerulli Associates, "Cerulli Anticipates $124 Trillion in Wealth Will Transfer Through 2048," December 5, 2024, *https://www.cerulli.com/press-releases /cerulli-anticipates-124-trillion-in-wealth-will-transfer-through-2048*.
2. Carnegie Corporation of New York, "Andrew Carnegie's Story," 2015, *www .carnegie.org/interactives/foundersstory*.
3. "Carnegie Libraries in Iowa Project," n.d., *https://carnegielibrariesiowa.org*.
4. PBS, "The Steel Business," *American Experience,* August 29, 2017, *www.pbs .org/wgbh/americanexperience/features/carnegie-steel-business*.
5. PBS, "The Strike at Homestead Mill," *American Experience,* August 29, 2017, *www.pbs.org/wgbh/americanexperience/features/carnegie-strike-homestead-mill*.
6. AFL-CIO, "1892 Homestead Strike," n.d., *https://aflcio.org/about/history/labor -history-events/1892-homestead-strike*.
7. AFL-CIO, "1892 Homestead Strike."
8. Andrew Carnegie, *The Gospel of Wealth* (1889; repr., New York: Carnegie Corporation of New York, 2017).
9. US National Park Service, "Carnegie Libraries: The Future Made Bright," Teaching with Historic Places program, n.d., *www.nps.gov/articles/carnegie -libraries-the-future-made-bright-teaching-with-historic-places.htm*.
10. Digital Public Library of America, "Segregated Libraries," September 2015, *https://dp.la/exhibitions/history-us-public-libraries/segregated-libraries*.
11. US National Park Service, "Carnegie Libraries."
12. Jacqui Shine, "Off The Books," *Lapham's Quarterly,* August 7, 2015, *www .laphamsquarterly.org/roundtable/books*.
13. Oxford Languages, under "gild."
14. Kimberly Hamlin, "The True History Behind HBO's 'The Gilded Age'," *Smithsonian Magazine,* January 20, 2022, *www.smithsonianmag.com/history /the-true-history-behind-hbos-the-gilded-age-180979415*.

15. Hamlin, "The True History Behind HBO's 'The Gilded Age'."
16. Foundation Mark, "Assets and Grantmaking Trends," June 2024, *https:// foundationmark.com/#/grants*.
17. Cerulli Associates, "Cerulli Anticipates $124 Trillion in Wealth Will Transfer Through 2048."
18. Ayana Elizabeth Johnson, *What If We Get It Right?: Visions of Climate Futures* (New York: One World, 2024).

Practice 1: Write a New Story

1. Harold R. Johnson, "Harold R. Johnson on How We Tell Our Own Stories," Literary Hub, October 24, 2022, *https://lithub.com/harold-r-johnson-on-how -we-tell-our-own-stories*.
2. William Dalrymple, "The Great Divide," *The New Yorker*, June 29, 2015, *www.newyorker.com/magazine/2015/06/29/the-great-divide-books-dalrymple*.
3. Susan King, "What I Learned About Donor Power From Trying to Hire Nikole Hannah-Jones," *Chronicle of Philanthropy*, January 9, 2024, *www .philanthropy.com/article/what-i-learned-about-donor-power-from-trying-to -hire-nikole-hannah-jones*.
4. Chuck Collins, Helen Flannery, Bella DeVaan, and Olivia Alperstein, "New Report From the Institute for Policy Studies Reveals the True Cost of Billion-aire Philanthropy," Institute for Policy Studies, November 15, 2023, *https:// ips-dc.org/release-new-report-from-the-institute-for-policy-studies-reveals-the-true -cost-of-billionaire-philanthropy*.
5. Carnegie, *Gospel of Wealth*.
6. Fannie Lou Hamer, "Speech Delivered at the Founding of the National Women's Political Caucus, Washington DC, July 10, 1971," in *The Speeches of Fannie Lou Hamer: To Tell It Like It Is,* ed. Maegan Parker Brooks and Davis W. Houck (Jackson, MS: University Press of Mississippi, 2011), 134–39, *www.jstor.org/stable/j.ctt12f641*.

Practice 2: Know Your History, So You Can Build the Future

1. PBS, "Biography: Andrew Carnegie," *American Experience,* August 29, 2017, *www.pbs.org/wgbh/americanexperience/features/carnegie-biography*.
2. Anupreeta Das, "Has The Long Friendship of Bill Gates and Warren Buffett Reached Its Final Act?," *New York Times,* August 4, 2024, *www.nytimes .com/2024/08/04/business/bill-gates-warren-buffett-friendship.html*.

3. All Carnegie quotes are from Carnegie, *Gospel of Wealth.*

4. Candid.org, "Key Facts on U.S. Nonprofits and Foundations," April 2020, *www.issuelab.org/resources/36381/36381.pdf.*

5. Rebecca Riddell, Nabil Ahmed, Alex Maitland, Max Lawson, and Anjela Taneja, "Inequality Inc.," Oxfam International, January 15, 2024, *www .oxfam.org/en/research/inequality-inc.*

6. Riddell et al., "Inequality Inc."

7. Neil Bhutta, Andrew C. Chang, Lisa J. Dettling, and Joanne W. Hsu, "Disparities in Wealth by Race and Ethnicity in the 2019 Survey of Consumer Finances," FEDS Notes, Board of Governors of the Federal Reserve System, September 28, 2020, *https://doi.org/10.17016/2380-7172.2797.*

8. Andre M. Perry, Hannah Stephens, and Manann Donoghoe, "Black Wealth Is Increasing, but So Is the Racial Wealth Gap," Brookings, January 9, 2024, *www.brookings.edu/articles/black-wealth-is-increasing-but-so-is-the-racial -wealth-gap.*

9. Bryan Stevenson, *Just Mercy: A Story of Justice and Redemption* (New York: Spiegel & Grau, 2014).

10. Sarina Dayal and Grace Sato, "Foundation Giving and Payout in 2022: What Changed and What's Next?," *Candid* (blog), June 29, 2023, *https://blog.candid .org/post/foundation-giving-and-payout-in-2022-what-changed-whats-next.*

11. Clifton R. Musser, "Letter from the Founder," September 6, 1946, General Service Foundation, *https://generalservice.org.*

12. Lally Weymouth, "Foundation Woes the Saga of Henry Ford II: Part Two," *New York Times,* March 12, 1978, *www.nytimes.com/1978/03/12/archives /foundation-woes-the-saga-of-henry-ford-ii-part-two-ford-ford.html.*

13. Weymouth, "Foundation Woes the Saga Of Henry Ford II."

14. Robert Griffin, Charlie Lobeck, Mariana Botero, Sarah Cooper, Michelle Diggles, Conor McKay, and Eliza Steffen, "Field in Focus: The State of Pro-Democracy Institutional Philanthropy," Democracy Fund, January 22, 2024, *https://democracyfund.org/idea/field-in-focus-the-state-of-pro-democracy -institutional-philanthropy.*

15. Brennan Center for Justice, "Voting Laws Roundup: 2023 in Review," January 18, 2024, *www.brennancenter.org/our-work/research-reports/voting-laws -roundup-2023-review.*

16. Brennan Center for Justice, "Fact Sheet: Growing Racial Disparities in Voter Turnout, 2008–2022," March 2, 2024, *www.brennancenter.org/our-work /research-reports/growing-racial-disparities-voter-turnout-2008-2022.*

17. Deepa Iyer, "Social Justice Nonprofits Facing Multiple Threats Need Solidarity and Support," Building Movement Project (blog), May 22, 2024, *https://buildingmovement.org/blog/threats-supports*.

18. Alex Daniels, "Will Giving Grants Based on Race Survive the Fearless Fund Case?," *Chronicle of Philanthropy*, June 26, 2024, *www.philanthropy.com/article/will-giving-grants-based-on-race-survive-the-fearless-fund-case*.

19. Michael Kavate, "'Transformation' at JPB Foundation: Eight Questions with Deepak Bhargava, President-Elect," *Inside Philanthropy*, September 18, 2023, *www.insidephilanthropy.com/home/2023/9/18/eight-questions-with-deepak-bhargava-jpb-foundation-president-elect*.

20. Miki Akimoto, "The Work of a Lifetime: Reparative Philanthropy, Relationships, Healing, and Joy," National Center for Family Philanthropy, November 16, 2022, *www.ncfp.org/2022/11/16/the-work-of-a-lifetime-reparative-philanthropy-relationships-healing-and-joy*.

21. Shellmound, "West Berkeley Shellmound Site to Return to Indigenous Stewardship," March 20, 2024, *https://shellmound.org/2024/03/shellmound-to-be-rematriated*.

22. Inés Ixierda, "Sogorea Te' Land Trust Receives $20 Million Shuumi Land Tax Contribution From Kataly Foundation," Sogorea Te' Land Trust, March 4, 2024, *https://sogoreate-landtrust.org/2024/03/04/sogorea-te-land-trust-receives-20-million-shuumi-land-tax-contribution-from-kataly-foundation*.

23. Heather McGhee, "Heather McGhee on Reparations as 'Seed Capital,'" *The. Ink* (blog), May 3, 2024, *https://the.ink/p/heather-mcghee-seed-capital-american-dream*.

24. Aria Florant, author interview, April 5, 2024.

25. Aria Florant, author interview, April 5, 2024.

26. Ahmad Abuznaid, Deepa Iyer, and Darakshan Raja, "We Need Movement Infrastructure," *Nonprofit Quarterly*, March 21, 2024, *https://nonprofitquarterly.org/we-need-movement-infrastructure*.

27. Farhad Ebrahimi, "How We Got Here," *Stanford Social Innovation Review*, Winter 2024, *https://doi.org/10.48558/1YTK-GA10*.

28. Calen Otto, "The Climate Funders Justice Pledge Holds Philanthropy Accountable," *Nonprofit Quarterly*, July 20, 2023, *https://nonprofitquarterly.org/the-climate-funders-justice-pledge-holds-philanthropy-accountable*.

29. Marion Gee and Gloria Walton, "Philanthropy Must Advance Climate Justice Now. Here's How," *Inside Philanthropy*, April 12, 2023, *www.insidephilanthropy.com/home/2023/4/12/philanthropy-must-advance-climate-justice-now-heres-how*.

30. Gee and Walton, "Philanthropy Must Advance Climate Justice Now."

31. Gee and Walton, "Philanthropy Must Advance Climate Justice Now."

32. Barbara Tomlinson and George Lipsitz, *Insubordinate Spaces: Improvisation and Accompaniment for Social Justice* (Philadelphia: Temple University Press, 2019), 29.

33. Vini Bhansali, author interview, March 1, 2024.

34. Rusty Stahl, "To Ensure Nonprofit Well-Being, Invest in Wages, Workload, and Working Conditions," Center for Effective Philanthropy (blog), June 6, 2024, *https://cep.org/blog/to-ensure-nonprofit-well-being-invest-in-wages-workload-and-working-conditions.*

Practice 3: Reimagine Governance

1. Patrick Butler, "UK Charity Foundation to Abolish Itself and Give Away £130m," *The Guardian,* July 11, 2023, *www.theguardian.com/society/2023/jul/11/uk-charity-foundation-to-abolish-itself-and-give-away-130m.*

2. Butler, "UK Charity Foundation to Abolish Itself."

3. Circle Forward, "Circle Forward FAQs," n.d., *https://circleforward.us/faqs.* Italics added.

4. Sandra J. Sucher and Shalene Gupta, "What Corporate Boards Can Learn from Boeing's Mistakes," *Harvard Business Review,* June 2, 2021, *https://hbr.org/2021/06/what-corporate-boards-can-learn-from-boeings-mistakes.*

5. Kerry Breen, "Florida's New Black History Curriculum Says 'Slaves Developed Skills' That Could Be Used for 'Personal Benefit'," CBS News, July 21, 2023, *www.cbsnews.com/news/floridas-new-education-standards-says-slavery-had-personal-benefits.*

6. Anne Wallestad, "The Four Principles of Purpose-Driven Board Leadership," *Stanford Social Innovation Review,* March 10, 2021, *https://doi.org/10.48558/S4ZJ-Q994.*

7. Rob Reich, *Just Giving: Why Philanthropy Is Failing Democracy and How It Can Do Better* (Princeton, NJ: Princeton University Press, 2018), 138.

8. Reich, *Just Giving,* 139.

9. Ellie Buteau and Jennifer Glickman, *Benchmarking Foundation Governance* (Center for Effective Philanthropy, October 2015), *https://cep.org/wp-content/uploads/2015/10/CEP_Benchmarking-Foundation-Governance_2015.pdf.*

10. Emerald Adeyemi and Don Chen, "Improving Philanthropic Practice by Prioritizing Reflection & Learning," National Center for Family Philanthropy, February 6, 2024, *www.ncfp.org/2024/02/06/improving-philanthropic-practice-by-prioritizing-reflection-learning.*

11. Adeyemi and Chen, "Improving Philanthropic Practice."

12. BoardSource, *Foundation Board Leadership: A Closer Look at Foundation Board Responses to "Leading with Intent 2017"* (BoardSource, 2019), *https://leading withintent.org/wp-content/uploads/2018/03/LWI2017-Foundations-Report.pdf.*

13. Kolibri Foundation, "Our Story," 2022, *https://kolibrifdn.org/our-story.*

14. Leah Hunt-Hendrix and Astra Taylor, *Solidarity: The Past, Present, and Future of a World-Changing Idea* (New York: Pantheon, 2024).

15. Hunt-Hendrix and Taylor, *Solidarity,* 136.

16. Farhad Ebrahimi, "Chorus Foundation Retrospective: A Q&A with Founder and Chair Farhad Ebrahimi," National Committee for Responsive Philanthropy, July 12, 2023, *https://ncrp.org/resources/responsive-philanthropy-summer-2023 /chorus-foundation-retrospective-a-qa-with-founder-and-chair-farhad-ebrahimi.*

17. *Merriam-Webster's Collegiate Dictionary* (2001), s.v. "stewardship."

18. F. B. Heron Foundation, "Investment Policy Statement," December 2017, *www.heron.org/wp-content/uploads/2018/07/IPS-2017-12.pdf.* Italics added.

19. National Philanthropic Trust, *2024 Donor-Advised Fund Report* (National Philanthropic Trust, 2024), *https://www.nptrust.org/wp-content/uploads/2024 /11/2024-DAF-Report-NPT.pdf.*

20. Bill & Melinda Gates Foundation, "Bill & Melinda Gates Foundation CEO Mark Suzman Announces Initial Plans to Evolve Governance as Bill Gates and Melinda French Gates Commit $15 Billion in New Resources to Deepen and Accelerate the Foundation's Efforts to Address Inequity," news release, July 7, 2021, *www.gatesfoundation.org/ideas/media-center/press-releases /2021/07/bill-melinda-gates-foundation-mark-suzman-plans-evolve-governance.*

21. Nicholas Kulish, "Three New Faces to Help Steer the Gates Foundation," *New York Times,* January 26, 2022, *www.nytimes.com/2022/01/26/business/gates -foundation-new-trustees.html.*

22. Julian Corner, personal communication, July 4, 2024.

Practice 4: Bend Time

1. Thalia Beaty, "In Unusual Push, Funders Band Together to Get Out Grants Around Election Work 'Early,'" AP News, April 30, 2024, *https://apnews.com /article/all-by-april-democracy-fund-tides-20baba159cde716e0d0f92129d4cc8f2.*

2. *Merriam-Webster's Collegiate Dictionary* (2001), s.v. "in perpetuity."

3. Reich, *Just Giving,* 57, quoting John Stuart Mill, *The Collected Works of John Stuart Mill, Volume IV, Essays on Economics and Society Part I,* ed. John M. Robson (Toronto: University of Toronto Press, 1967).

4. Dayal and Sato, "Foundation Giving and Payout in 2022."

5. Some foundations use a three-year rolling average value of their endowments when they are calculating spending, in order to smooth the impact of sudden increases or declines. This methodology keeps spending from dropping suddenly when markets drop, but the effect of a decline in assets is still felt by grantees, just at a later date.

6. Dimple Abichandani, "A 'Balancing Test' for Foundation Spending," *Stanford Social Innovation Review,* February 10, 2020, *https://doi.org/10.48558/JAY0 -9A73.*

7. Solidaire Network: A Donor Network for Radical Philanthropy, *https:// solidairenetwork.org.*

8. Mia Birdsong, *How We Show Up: Reclaiming Family, Friendship, and Community* (New York: Hachette Go, 2020); Mia Birdsong and Saneta deVuono-powell, *Freedom's Revival: Research from the Headwaters of Liberation* (Oakland, CA: Next River, 2023).

9. Mia Birdsong, personal communication, April 23, 2024.

10. Jamie Allison, author interview, March 29, 2024.

11. Jamie Allison, author interview, March 29, 2024.

12. Rachel Morford, "Obituary: Hope Lewis, Northeastern Law Professor, Remembered as Passionate Human Rights Scholar," *Huntington News,* December 9, 2016, *https://huntnewsnu.com/45494/campus/obituary-hope-lewis -northeastern-law-professor-remembered-as-passionate-human-rights-scholar*; Randall Robinson, *The Debt: What America Owes to Blacks* (New York: Plume, 2001).

13. David Brooks, "The Case for Reparations," *New York Times,* March 7, 2019, *www.nytimes.com/2019/03/07/opinion/case-for-reparations.html.*

14. Ta-Nehisi Coates, "The Case for Reparations," *The Atlantic,* June 2014, *www.theatlantic.com/magazine/archive/2014/06/the-case-for-reparations /361631.*

15. Nikole Hannah-Jones, "The 1619 Project," *New York Times,* August 14, 2019, *www.nytimes.com/interactive/2019/08/14/magazine/1619-america-slavery.html.*

Practice 5: Follow the Money

1. Philip Rojc, "What Is 'Risk' in Philanthropy, and Are We Still Giving Funders Too Much Credit for It?," *Inside Philanthropy,* March 28, 2024, *www.insidephilanthropy.com/home/2024/3/28/what-is-risk-in-philanthropy -and-are-we-still-giving-funders-too-much-credit-for-it.*

2. Michael Kavate, "Six Questions with Ellen Dorsey, Who Helped Convince Philanthropies to Divest," *Inside Philanthropy*, March 11, 2024, *www.insidephilanthropy.com/home/2024/3/11/six-questions-with-ellen-dorsey-who-helped-convince-philanthropies-to-divest*.

3. Lem White and Keiko Murase, "Building Power, Building Wealth: The Value of Community-Driven Models," *Nonprofit Quarterly*, June 22, 2022, *https://nonprofitquarterly.org/building-power-building-wealth-the-value-of-community-driven-models*.

Practice 6: Embody Change

1. Eveline Shen, author interview, April 4, 2024.

2. Sheryl Petty, Kristen Zimmerman, and Mark Leach, "Toward Love, Healing, Resilience & Alignment: The Inner Work of Social Transformation & Justice," *Nonprofit Quarterly*, May 12, 2017, *https://nonprofitquarterly.org/toward-love-healing-resilience-alignment-inner-work-social-transformation-justice*.

3. Eveline Shen, "The Courageous Operating System," Leading Courageously, n.d., *https://leadingcourageously.com*.

4. Dimple Abichandani, "Pandemic Philanthropy: Moving from Relief to Power," *Inside Philanthropy*, May 7, 2020, *www.insidephilanthropy.com/home/2020/5/7/pandemic-philanthropy-moving-from-relief-to-power*.

5. Author interview with an anonymous grantseeker.

6. Borealis Philanthropy, "The Disability Inclusion Fund Awards $400K in Joy Grants to Disabled-Led Organizers, Emphasizing Well-Being as Essential to Our Collective Liberation," news release, December 6, 2023, *https://borealisphilanthropy.org/2023/12/06/the-disability-inclusion-fund-awards-400k-in-joy-grants-to-disabled-led-organizers-emphasizing-well-being-as-essential-to-our-collective-liberation*.

7. Sandy Ho, personal communication, August 9,2024.

8. Daniels, "Will Giving Grants Based on Race Survive the Fearless Fund Case?"

9. Yanique Redwood, *White Women Cry & Call Me Angry: A Black Woman's Memoir on Racism in Philanthropy* (self-pub., 2023), *www.whitewomencry.com*.

10. "Stop Drowning Us, and Stop Making Us Disappear: A Critical Report on the State of Black Woman Leadership," *Nonprofit Quarterly*, Spring 2024, *https://store.nonprofitquarterly.org/products/stop-drowning-us-and-stop-making-us-disappear-a-critical-report-on-the-state-of-black-woman-leadership-spring-2024-print-issue*.

11. Tomlinson and Lipsitz, *Insubordinate Spaces*, 1.

Practice 7: Identify and Replace Philanthropic Artifacts

1. The Styles Desk, "Gen Z-ers and Millennials React to 'L.A. Law'," *New York Times,* November 23, 2023, *www.nytimes.com/2023/11/23/style/la-law-hulu.html.*

2. Faster Than 20, *https://fasterthan20.com.*

3. adrienne maree brown, *Emergent Strategy: Shaping Change, Changing Worlds* (Chico, CA: AK Press, 2017), 3.

4. Jara Dean-Coffey, personal communication, June 28, 2024.

5. Equitable Evaluation Initiative, *Shifting the Evaluation Paradigm: The Equitable Evaluation Framework,* (Grantmakers for Effective Organizations, April 30, 2021), *www.geofunders.org/resources/shifting-the-evaluation-paradigm-the -equitable-evaluation-framework.*

6. Jara Dean-Coffey, personal communication, June 28, 2024.

Practice 8: Fund Complexity and Wholeness

1. Ellen Bravo, "Respect the Bump Gets Results as Well as Respect," *The Blog, HuffPost,* September 29, 2014, *www.huffpost.com/entry/respect-the-bump -gets-res_b_5881338.*

2. "How Many People Work at Walmart?," Walmart, n.d., *https://corporate.walmart .com/askwalmart/how-many-people-work-at-walmart.*

3. Caroline Picker, author interview, May 24, 2024.

4. Caroline Picker, author interview, May 24, 2024.

5. Rockefeller Philanthropy Advisors, "Your Philanthropy Roadmap," October 18, 2017, *www.rockpa.org/wp-content/uploads/2017/08/Your-Philanthropy -Roadmap.pdf.*

6. Patrick Strickland, "US: Are 'anti-Sharia' bills legalising Islamophobia?," Al Jazeera, October 1, 2017, *www.aljazeera.com/news/2017/10/1/us-are-anti -sharia-bills-legalising-islamophobia.*

7. Ryan H. Boyer, "'Unveiling' Kansas's Ban on Application of Foreign Law," *Kansas Law Review* 61 (2013), 1061–87, *https://kuscholarworks.ku.edu /bitstream/handle/1808/20237/Boyer.pdf.*

8. Trans Legislation Tracker, "Tracking the Rise of Anti-trans Bills in the U.S.," n.d., *https://translegislation.com/learn.*

9. Kimberlee Kruesi and Jonathan Mattise, "Tennessee's House Expels 2 of 3 Democrats Over Guns Protest," AP News, April 7, 2023, *https://apnews.com /article/tennessee-lawmakers-expulsion-d3f40559c56a051eec49e416a7b5dade.*

10. National Partnership for Women & Families, "Leading on Leave: Companies with New or Expanded Paid Leave Policies (2015–2020)," 2020,

https://nationalpartnership.org/wp-content/uploads/2023/02/new-and-expanded-employer-paid-family-leave-policies.pdf.

11. Natalie Bennett, "We Do Not Live Single-Issue Lives," Women's Leadership and Resource Center, University of Illinois Chicago, March 1, 2023, *https://wlrc.uic.edu/news-stories/we-do-not-live-single-issue-lives.*

12. Columbia Law School, "Kimberlé Crenshaw on Intersectionality, More Than Two Decades Later," June 8, 2017, *www.law.columbia.edu/news/archive/kimberle-crenshaw-intersectionality-more-two-decades-later.*

Practice 9: See Opportunity in Every Crisis

1. World Economic Forum, *Global Risks Report 2023: Insight Report* (Geneva, Switzerland: World Economic Forum, January 11, 2023), *www3.weforum.org/docs/WEF_Global_Risks_Report_2023.pdf*; Daniel Drezner, "Are We Headed Toward a 'Polycrisis'? The Buzzword of the Moment, Explained," *Vox,* January 28, 2023, *www.vox.com/23572710/polycrisis-davos-history-climate-russia-ukraine-inflation.*

2. World Economic Forum, *Global Risks Report 2023.*

3. Adia Colar and Yna Moore, "New Report Finds at Least $1B Given by Philanthropy for COVID-19 in 2021," Candid, May 25, 2022, *https://candid.org/about/press-room/releases/new-report-finds-at-least-1b-given-by-philanthropy-for-covid-19-in-2021.*

4. Naomi Klein, "A New Shock Doctrine: In a World of Crisis, Morality Can Still Win," *The Guardian,* September 28, 2017, *www.theguardian.com/commentisfree/2017/sep/28/labour-shock-doctrine-moral-strategy-naomi-klein.*

5. Klein, "A New Shock Doctrine."

6. Crystal Hayling and Daniel Lau, email message to author, June 28, 2024.

7. Daniel Lau, author interview, May 21, 2024.

8. Daniel Lau, author interview, May 21, 2024.

9. World Economic Forum, *Global Risks Report 2023,* fig. C, *www3.weforum.org/docs/WEF_Global_Risks_Report_2023.pdf#page=10.*

Practice 10: All Together Now

1. Candid.org, "Key Facts on U.S. Nonprofits and Foundations"; Observatoire de la Fondation de France, "An Overview of Philanthropy in Europe," April 2015, *www.fondationdefrance.org/images/pdf/Philanthropy_in_Europe_april_2015.pdf.*

2. My gratitude to Eugene Kim (*https://fasterthan20.com*), who first shared this image with me of people on a tandem bike biking in different directions to explain why sometimes different people working on the same thing doesn't result in forward momentum.

3. Cerulli Associates, "Cerulli Anticipates $124 Trillion in Wealth Will Transfer Through 2048."

4. Alison Powell, Simon Morfit, and Michael John, "Releasing the Potential of Philanthropic Collaborations," Bridgespan Group, December 14, 2021, *www.bridgespan.org/getmedia/5590afe6-fe08-452e-9afd-bedfbc586cf6/releasing -the-potential-of-philanthropic-collaborations-2021.pdf*.

5. Maria Di Mento and Jim Rendon, "Who's Up Next? How the Next Wave of Megadonors Will Give," *Chronicle of Philanthropy,* March 5, 2024, *www .philanthropy.com/article/whos-up-next-how-the-next-wave-of-megadonors-will-give*.

6. Di Mento and Rendon, "Who's Up Next?"

7. Neighborhood Funders Group, "Amplify Fund," n.d., *https://nfg.org/program /amplify*; The Partnership Fund, "Building Power in Community," March 15, 2023, *www.thepartnershipfund.net*.

8. Adriana Loson-Ceballos and Michael D. Layton, "In Abundance: An Analysis of the Thriving Landscape of Collective Giving in the U.S.," Dorothy A. Johnson Center for Philanthropy, *https://johnsoncenter.org/wp-content/uploads /2024/04/in-abundance-an-analysis-of-the-thriving-landscape-of-collective -giving-in-the-u-s.pdf*.

9. Isis Krause and Sara Lomelin, author interview, March 19, 2024.

10. Loson-Ceballos and Layton, "In Abundance."

11. Melinda French Gates, "The Enemies of Progress Play Offense. I Want to Help Even the Match," *New York Times,* May 28, 2024, *www.nytimes.com /2024/05/28/opinion/melinda-french-gates-reproductive-rights.html*.

12. Powell, Morfit, and John, "Releasing the Potential of Philanthropic Collaborations."

13. Powell, Morfit, and John, "Releasing the Potential of Philanthropic Collaborations."

14. Jennifer Stout, author interview, March 6, 2024.

15. Bridgit Antoinette Evans, author interview, March 4, 2024.

16. Shaady Salehi, personal communication.

17. Iara Peng, author interview, March 25, 2024.

18. Isis Krause and Sara Lomelin, author interview, March 19, 2024.

Acknowledgments and Gratitudes

1. Timothy Snyder, *On Tyranny: Twenty Lessons from the Twentieth Century* (New York: Random House, 2017).

2. Patricia J. Williams, *The Alchemy of Race and Rights: Diary of a Law Professor* (Cambridge, MA: Harvard University Press, 1991).

3. INCITE! Women of Color Against Violence, *The Revolution Will Not Be Funded: Beyond the Nonprofit Industrial Complex* (Durham, NC: Duke University Press, 2017); Edgar Villanueva, *Decolonizing Wealth: Indigenous Wisdom to Heal Divides and Restore Balance* (Oakland, CA: Berrett-Koehler, 2018); Anand Giridharadas, *Winners Take All: The Elite Charade of Changing the World* (London: Penguin, 2019).

BIBLIOGRAPHY

Abichandani, Dimple. "A 'Balancing Test' for Foundation Spending." *Stanford Social Innovation Review.* February 10, 2020. *https://doi.org/10.48558 /JAY0-9A73.*

Abichandani, Dimple. "Pandemic Philanthropy: Moving from Relief to Power." *Inside Philanthropy.* May 7, 2020. *www.insidephilanthropy.com/home/2020/5 /7/pandemic-philanthropy-moving-from-relief-to-power.*

Abuznaid, Ahmad, Deepa Iyer, and Darakshan Raja. "We Need Movement Infrastructure." *Nonprofit Quarterly.* March 21, 2024. *https://nonprofitquarterly .org/we-need-movement-infrastructure.*

Adeyemi, Emerald, and Don Chen. "Improving Philanthropic Practice by Prioritizing Reflection & Learning." National Center for Family Philanthropy. February 6, 2024. *www.ncfp.org/2024/02/06/improving-philanthropic -practice-by-prioritizing-reflection-learning.*

AFL-CIO. "1892 Homestead Strike." N.d. *https://aflcio.org/about/history/labor -history-events/1892-homestead-strike.*

Agbo, Nwamaka. "Progress Is Won by Pursuing Justice, Not Waiting Patiently in Line." *Chronicle of Philanthropy.* June 18, 2024. *www.philanthropy.com /commons/progress-is-won-by-pursuing-justice-not-waiting-patiently-in-line.*

Akimoto, Miki. "The Work of a Lifetime: Reparative Philanthropy, Relationships, Healing, and Joy." National Center for Family Philanthropy. November 16, 2022. *www.ncfp.org/2022/11/16/the-work-of-a-lifetime-reparative-philanthropy -relationships-healing-and-joy.*

Beaty, Thalia. "In Unusual Push, Funders Band Together to Get Out Grants Around Election Work 'Early.'" AP News. April 30, 2024. *https://apnews.com /article/all-by-april-democracy-fund-tides-20baba159cde716e0d0f92129d4cc8f2.*

Bennett, Natalie. "We Do Not Live Single-Issue Lives." Women's Leadership and Resource Center, University of Illinois Chicago. March 1, 2023. *https://wlrc .uic.edu/news-stories/we-do-not-live-single-issue-lives.*

Bhutta, Neil, Andrew C. Chang, Lisa J. Dettling, and Joanne W. Hsu. "Disparities in Wealth by Race and Ethnicity in the 2019 Survey of Consumer Finances." FEDS Notes. Board of Governors of the Federal Reserve System. September 28, 2020. *https://doi.org/10.17016/2380-7172.2797.*

Bill & Melinda Gates Foundation. "Bill & Melinda Gates Foundation CEO Mark Suzman Announces Initial Plans to Evolve Governance as Bill Gates and Melinda French Gates Commit $15 Billion in New Resources to Deepen and Accelerate the Foundation's Efforts to Address Inequity." News release. July 7, 2021. *www.gatesfoundation.org/ideas/media-center/press -releases/2021/07/bill-melinda-gates-foundation-mark-suzman-plans-evolve -governance.*

Birdsong, Mia. *How We Show Up: Reclaiming Family, Friendship, and Community.* New York: Hachette Go, 2020.

Birdsong, Mia, and Saneta deVuono-powell. *Freedom's Revival: Research from the Headwaters of Liberation.* Oakland, CA: Next River, 2023.

BoardSource. *Foundation Board Leadership: A Closer Look at Foundation Board Responses to "Leading with Intent 2017."* BoardSource. 2019. *https://leading withintent.org/wp-content/uploads/2018/03/LWI2017-Foundations-Report.pdf.*

Borealis Philanthropy. "The Disability Inclusion Fund Awards $400K in Joy Grants to Disabled-Led Organizers, Emphasizing Well-Being as Essential to Our Collective Liberation." News release. December 6, 2023. *https:// borealisphilanthropy.org/2023/12/06/the-disability-inclusion-fund-awards-400k -in-joy-grants-to-disabled-led-organizers-emphasizing-well-being-as-essential -to-our-collective-liberation.*

Boyer, Ryan H. "'Unveiling' Kansas's Ban on Application of Foreign Law." *Kansas Law Review* 61 (2013), 1061–87. *https://kuscholarworks.ku.edu/bitstream /handle/1808/20237/Boyer.pdf.*

Bravo, Ellen. "Respect the Bump Gets Results as Well as Respect." *The Blog.* *HuffPost.* September 29, 2014. *www.huffpost.com/entry/respect-the-bump-gets -res_b_5881338.*

Breen, Kerry. "Florida's New Black History Curriculum Says 'Slaves Developed Skills' That Could Be Used for 'Personal Benefit'." CBS News. July 21, 2023.

www.cbsnews.com/news/floridas-new-education-standards-says-slavery
-had-personal-benefits.

Brennan Center for Justice. "Fact Sheet: Growing Racial Disparities in Voter
Turnout, 2008–2022." March 2, 2024. www.brennancenter.org/our-work
/research-reports/growing-racial-disparities-voter-turnout-2008-2022.

Brennan Center for Justice. "Voting Laws Roundup: 2023 in Review." January 18, 2024. www.brennancenter.org/our-work/research-reports/voting-laws
-roundup-2023-review.

Brooks, David. "The Case for Reparations." *New York Times.* March 7, 2019.
www.nytimes.com/2019/03/07/opinion/case-for-reparations.html.

brown, adrienne maree. *Emergent Strategy: Shaping Change, Changing Worlds.*
Chico, CA: AK Press, 2017.

Buteau, Ellie, and Jennifer Glickman. *Benchmarking Foundation Governance.*
Center for Effective Philanthropy. October 2015. https://cep.org/wp-content
/uploads/2015/10/CEP_Benchmarking-Foundation-Governance_2015.pdf.

Butler, Patrick. "UK Charity Foundation to Abolish Itself and Give Away
£130m." *The Guardian.* July 11, 2023. www.theguardian.com/society/2023
/jul/11/uk-charity-foundation-to-abolish-itself-and-give-away-130m.

Candid.org. "Key Facts on U.S. Nonprofits and Foundations." April 2020.
www.issuelab.org/resources/36381/36381.pdf.

Carnegie, Andrew. *The Gospel of Wealth.* New York: Carnegie Corporation of
New York, 2017. First published 1889.

Carnegie Corporation of New York. "Andrew Carnegie's Story." 2015. www
.carnegie.org/interactives/foundersstory.

Cerulli Associates. "Cerulli Anticipates $124 Trillion in Wealth Will Transfer
Through 2048." December 5, 2024. https://www.cerulli.com/press-releases
/cerulli-anticipates-124-trillion-in-wealth-will-transfer-through-2048.

Coates, Ta-Nehisi. "The Case for Reparations." *The Atlantic.* June 2014. www
.theatlantic.com/magazine/archive/2014/06/the-case-for-reparations/361631.

Colar, Adia, and Yna Moore. "New Report Finds at Least $1B Given by Philanthropy for COVID-19 in 2021." Candid. May 25, 2022. https://candid.org
/about/press-room/releases/new-report-finds-at-least-1b-given-by-philanthropy-for
-covid-19-in-2021.

Collins, Chuck, Helen Flannery, Bella DeVaan, and Olivia Alperstein. "New
Report From the Institute for Policy Studies Reveals the True Cost of Billionaire Philanthropy." Institute for Policy Studies. November 15, 2023. https://
ips-dc.org/release-new-report-from-the-institute-for-policy-studies-reveals-the-true
-cost-of-billionaire-philanthropy.

Columbia Law School. "Kimberlé Crenshaw on Intersectionality, More Than Two Decades Later." June 8, 2017. *www.law.columbia.edu/news/archive /kimberle-crenshaw-intersectionality-more-two-decades-later.*

Dalrymple, William. "The Great Divide." *The New Yorker.* June 29, 2015. *www .newyorker.com/magazine/2015/06/29/the-great-divide-books-dalrymple.*

Daniels, Alex. "Will Giving Grants Based on Race Survive the Fearless Fund Case?" *Chronicle of Philanthropy.* June 26, 2024. *www.philanthropy.com/article /will-giving-grants-based-on-race-survive-the-fearless-fund-case.*

Das, Anupreeta. "Has The Long Friendship of Bill Gates and Warren Buffett Reached Its Final Act?" *New York Times.* August 4, 2024. *www.nytimes.com /2024/08/04/business/bill-gates-warren-buffett-friendship.html.*

Dayal, Sarina, and Grace Sato. "Foundation Giving and Payout in 2022: What Changed and What's Next?" *Candid* (blog). June 29, 2023. *https://blog.candid .org/post/foundation-giving-and-payout-in-2022-what-changed-whats-next.*

Di Mento, Maria, and Jim Rendon. "Who's Up Next? How the Next Wave of Megadonors Will Give." *Chronicle of Philanthropy.* March 5, 2024. *www .philanthropy.com/article/whos-up-next-how-the-next-wave-of-megadonors -will-give.*

Digital Public Library of America. "Segregated Libraries." N.d. *https://dp.la /exhibitions/history-us-public-libraries/segregated-libraries.*

Drezner, Daniel. "Are We Headed Toward a 'Polycrisis'? The Buzzword of the Moment, Explained." *Vox.* January 28, 2023. *www.vox.com/23572710 /polycrisis-davos-history-climate-russia-ukraine-inflation.*

Ebrahimi, Farhad. "Chorus Foundation Retrospective: A Q&A with Founder and Chair Farhad Ebrahimi." National Committee for Responsive Philanthropy. July 12, 2023. *https://ncrp.org/resources/responsive-philanthropy-summer-2023 /chorus-foundation-retrospective-a-qa-with-founder-and-chair-farhad-ebrahimi.*

Ebrahimi, Farhad. "How We Got Here." *Stanford Social Innovation Review.* Winter 2024. *https://doi.org/10.48558/1YTK-GA10.*

Equitable Evaluation Initiative. *Shifting the Evaluation Paradigm: The Equitable Evaluation Framework.* Report. Grantmakers for Effective Organizations. April 30, 2021. *www.geofunders.org/resources/shifting-the-evaluation-paradigm -the-equitable-evaluation-framework.*

F. B. Heron Foundation. "Investment Policy Statement." December 2017. *www.heron.org/wp-content/uploads/2018/07/IPS-2017-12.pdf.*

Flannery, Helen. "Private Foundations Gave $2.6 Billion in Grants to National Donor-Advised Funds in 2021." Inequality.org. July 6, 2023. *https:// inequality.org/great-divide/private-foundations-dafs-2021.*

Foundation Mark. "Assets and Grantmaking Trends." June 2024. *https://foundationmark.com/#/grants.*

Gates, Melinda French. "The Enemies of Progress Play Offense. I Want to Help Even the Match." *New York Times.* May 28, 2024. *www.nytimes.com/2024/05/28/opinion/melinda-french-gates-reproductive-rights.html.*

Gee, Marion, and Gloria Walton. "Philanthropy Must Advance Climate Justice Now. Here's How." *Inside Philanthropy.* April 12, 2023. *www.insidephilanthropy.com/home/2023/4/12/philanthropy-must-advance-climate-justice-now-heres-how.*

Giridharadas, Anand. *Winners Take All: The Elite Charade of Changing the World.* London: Penguin, 2019.

Griffin, Robert, Charlie Lobeck, Mariana Botero, Sarah Cooper, Michelle Diggles, Conor McKay, and Eliza Steffen. "Field in Focus: The State of Pro-Democracy Institutional Philanthropy." Democracy Fund. January 22, 2024. *https://democracyfund.org/idea/field-in-focus-the-state-of-pro-democracy-institutional-philanthropy.*

Hamer, Fannie Lou. "Speech Delivered at the Founding of the National Women's Political Caucus, Washington DC, July 10, 1971." In *The Speeches of Fannie Lou Hamer: To Tell It Like It Is.* Edited by Maegan Parker Brooks and Davis W. Houck, 134–39. Jackson, MS: University Press of Mississippi, 2011. *www.jstor.org/stable/j.ctt12f641.*

Hamlin, Kimberly. "The True History Behind HBO's 'The Gilded Age'." *Smithsonian Magazine.* January 20, 2022. *www.smithsonianmag.com/history/the-true-history-behind-hbos-the-gilded-age-180979415.*

Hannah-Jones, Nikole. "The 1619 Project." *New York Times.* August 14, 2019. *www.nytimes.com/interactive/2019/08/14/magazine/1619-america-slavery.html.*

Harjo, Joy. *Catching the Light.* New Haven, CT: Yale University Press, 2022.

Hunt-Hendrix, Leah, and Astra Taylor. *Solidarity: The Past, Present, and Future of a World-Changing Idea.* New York: Pantheon, 2024.

INCITE! Women of Color Against Violence. *The Revolution Will Not Be Funded: Beyond the Nonprofit Industrial Complex.* Durham, NC: Duke University Press, 2017.

Ixierda, Inés. "Sogorea Te' Land Trust Receives $20 Million Shuumi Land Tax Contribution From Kataly Foundation." Sogorea Te' Land Trust. March 4, 2024. *https://sogoreate-landtrust.org/2024/03/04/sogorea-te-land-trust-receives-20-million-shuumi-land-tax-contribution-from-kataly-foundation.*

Iyer, Deepa. "Social Justice Nonprofits Facing Multiple Threats Need Solidarity and Support." Building Movement Project (blog). May 22, 2024. *https://buildingmovement.org/blog/threats-supports.*

Johnson, Ayana Elizabeth. *What If We Get It Right?: Visions of Climate Futures.* New York: One World, 2024.

Johnson, Harold R. "Harold R. Johnson on How We Tell Our Own Stories." *Literary Hub.* October 24, 2022. *https://lithub.com/harold-r-johnson-on-how -we-tell-our-own-stories.*

Kavate, Michael. "Six Questions with Ellen Dorsey, Who Helped Convince Philanthropies to Divest." *Inside Philanthropy.* March 11, 2024. *www.inside philanthropy.com/home/2024/3/11/six-questions-with-ellen-dorsey-who-helped -convince-philanthropies-to-divest.*

Kavate, Michael. "'Transformation' at JPB Foundation: Eight Questions with Deepak Bhargava, President-Elect." *Inside Philanthropy.* September 18, 2023. *www.insidephilanthropy.com/home/2023/9/18/eight-questions-with-deepak -bhargava-jpb-foundation-president-elect.*

King, Susan. "What I Learned About Donor Power From Trying to Hire Nikole Hannah-Jones." *Chronicle of Philanthropy.* January 9, 2024. *www .philanthropy.com/article/what-i-learned-about-donor-power-from-trying -to-hire-nikole-hannah-jones.*

Klein, Naomi. "A New Shock Doctrine: In a World of Crisis, Morality Can Still Win." *The Guardian.* September 28, 2017. *www.theguardian.com/commentisfree /2017/sep/28/labour-shock-doctrine-moral-strategy-naomi-klein.*

Kolibri Foundation. "Our Story." 2022. *https://kolibrifdn.org/our-story.*

Kruesi, Kimberlee, and Jonathan Mattise. "Tennessee's House Expels 2 of 3 Democrats Over Guns Protest." AP News. April 7, 2023. *https://apnews.com /article/tennessee-lawmakers-expulsion-d3f40559c56a051eec49e416a7b5dade.*

Kulish, Nicholas. "Three New Faces to Help Steer the Gates Foundation." *New York Times.* January 26, 2022. *www.nytimes.com/2022/01/26/business/gates -foundation-new-trustees.html.*

Loson-Ceballos, Adriana, and Michael D. Layton. "In Abundance: An Analysis of the Thriving Landscape of Collective Giving in the U.S." Dorothy A. Johnson Center for Philanthropy. *https://johnsoncenter.org/wp-content/uploads /2024/04/in-abundance-an-analysis-of-the-thriving-landscape-of-collective -giving-in-the-u-s.pdf.*

McGhee, Heather. "Heather McGhee on Reparations as 'Seed Capital.'" *The.Ink* (blog). May 3, 2024. *https://the.ink/p/heather-mcghee-seed-capital-american-dream.*

Mill, John Stuart. *The Collected Works of John Stuart Mill, Volume IV, Essays on Economics and Society Part I.* Edited by John M. Robson. Toronto: University of Toronto Press, 1967.

Morford, Rachel. "Obituary: Hope Lewis, Northeastern Law Professor, Remembered as Passionate Human Rights Scholar." *Huntington News.* December 9, 2016. *https://huntnewsnu.com/45494/campus/obituary-hope-lewis-northeastern-law-professor-remembered-as-passionate-human-rights-scholar.*

Musser, Clifton R. "Letter from the Founder" September 6, 1946. General Service Foundation. *https://generalservice.org.*

National Partnership for Women & Families. "Leading on Leave: Companies with New or Expanded Paid Leave Policies (2015–2020)." 2020. *https://nationalpartnership.org/wp-content/uploads/2023/02/new-and-expanded-employer-paid-family-leave-policies.pdf.*

National Philanthropic Trust. *2024 Donor-Advised Fund Report.* National Philanthropic Trust. 2024. *https://www.nptrust.org/wp-content/uploads/2024/11/2024-DAF-Report-NPT.pdf.*

Neighborhood Funders Group. "Amplify Fund." N.d. *https://nfg.org/program/amplify.*

Nonprofit Quarterly. "Stop Drowning Us, and Stop Making Us Disappear: A Critical Report on the State of Black Woman Leadership." *Nonprofit Quarterly.* Spring 2024. *https://store.nonprofitquarterly.org/products/stop-drowning-us-and-stop-making-us-disappear-a-critical-report-on-the-state-of-black-woman-leadership-spring-2024-print-issue.*

Observatoire de la Fondation de France. "An Overview of Philanthropy in Europe." April 2015. *www.fondationdefrance.org/images/pdf/Philanthropy_in_Europe_april_2015.pdf.*

Otto, Calen. "The Climate Funders Justice Pledge Holds Philanthropy Accountable." *Nonprofit Quarterly.* July 20, 2023. *https://nonprofitquarterly.org/the-climate-funders-justice-pledge-holds-philanthropy-accountable.*

Partnership Fund. "Building Power in Community." March 15, 2023. *www.thepartnershipfund.net.*

PBS. "Biography: Andrew Carnegie." *American Experience.* August 29, 2017. *www.pbs.org/wgbh/americanexperience/features/carnegie-biography.*

PBS. "The Steel Business." *American Experience.* August 29, 2017. *www.pbs.org/wgbh/americanexperience/features/carnegie-steel-business.*

PBS. "The Strike at Homestead Mill." *American Experience.* August 29, 2017. *www.pbs.org/wgbh/americanexperience/features/carnegie-strike-homestead-mill.*

Perry, Andre M., Hannah Stephens, and Manann Donoghoe. "Black Wealth Is Increasing, but So Is the Racial Wealth Gap." Brookings. January 9, 2024. *www.brookings.edu/articles/black-wealth-is-increasing-but-so-is-the-racial-wealth-gap.*

Petty, Sheryl, Kristen Zimmerman, and Mark Leach. "Toward Love, Healing, Resilience & Alignment: The Inner Work of Social Transformation & Justice." *Nonprofit Quarterly.* May 12, 2017. *https://nonprofitquarterly.org/toward -love-healing-resilience-alignment-inner-work-social-transformation-justice.*

Philanthropy Roundtable. "Statistics on U.S. Generosity." November 20, 2023. *https://www.philanthropyroundtable.org/almanac/statistics-on-u-s-generosity/.*

Powell, Alison, Simon Morfit, and Michael John. "Releasing the Potential of Philanthropic Collaborations." Bridgespan Group. December 14, 2021. *www.bridgespan.org/getmedia/5590afe6-fe08-452e-9afd-bedfbc586cf6/releasing -the-potential-of-philanthropic-collaborations-2021.pdf.*

Redwood, Yanique. *White Women Cry & Call Me Angry: A Black Woman's Memoir on Racism in Philanthropy.* Self-published, 2023. *www.whitewomencry.com.*

Reich, Rob. *Just Giving: Why Philanthropy Is Failing Democracy and How It Can Do Better.* Princeton, NJ: Princeton University Press, 2018.

Riddell, Rebecca, Nabil Ahmed, Alex Maitland, Max Lawson, and Anjela Taneja. "Inequality Inc." Oxfam International. January 15, 2024. *www.oxfam.org/en /research/inequality-inc.*

Robinson, Randall. *The Debt: What America Owes to Blacks.* New York: Plume, 2001.

Rockefeller Philanthropy Advisors. "Your Philanthropy Roadmap." October 18, 2017. *www.rockpa.org/wp-content/uploads/2017/08/Your-Philanthropy -Roadmap.pdf.*

Rojc, Philip. "What Is 'Risk' in Philanthropy, and Are We Still Giving Funders Too Much Credit for It?" *Inside Philanthropy.* March 28, 2024. *www .insidephilanthropy.com/home/2024/3/28/what-is-risk-in-philanthropy-and-are -we-still-giving-funders-too-much-credit-for-it.*

Shellmound. "West Berkeley Shellmound Site to Return to Indigenous Steward-ship." March 20, 2024. *https://shellmound.org/2024/03/shellmound-to-be -rematriated.*

Shen, Eveline. "The Courageous Operating System." Leading Courageously. N.d. *https://leadingcourageously.com.*

Shine, Jacqui. "Off The Books." *Lapham's Quarterly.* August 7, 2015. *www .laphamsquarterly.org/roundtable/books.*

Snyder, Timothy. *On Tyranny: Twenty Lessons from the Twentieth Century.* New York: Random House, 2017.

Solidaire Network: A Donor Network for Radical Philanthropy. *https://solidaire network.org.*

Stahl, Rusty. "To Ensure Nonprofit Well-Being, Invest in Wages, Workload, and Working Conditions." Center for Effective Philanthropy (blog). June 6, 2024. *https://cep.org/blog/to-ensure-nonprofit-well-being-invest-in-wages-workload-and-working-conditions.*

Stevenson, Bryan. *Just Mercy: A Story of Justice and Redemption.* New York: Spiegel & Grau, 2014.

Strickland, Patrick. "US: Are 'anti-Sharia' bills legalising Islamophobia?" Al Jazeera. October 1, 2017. *www.aljazeera.com/news/2017/10/1/us-are-anti-sharia-bills-legalising-islamophobia.*

Styles Desk. "Gen Z-ers and Millennials React to 'L.A. Law'." *New York Times.* November 23, 2023. *www.nytimes.com/2023/11/23/style/la-law-hulu.html.*

Sucher, Sandra J., and Shalene Gupta. "What Corporate Boards Can Learn from Boeing's Mistakes." *Harvard Business Review.* June 2, 2021. *https://hbr.org/2021/06/what-corporate-boards-can-learn-from-boeings-mistakes.*

Tomlinson, Barbara, and George Lipsitz. *Insubordinate Spaces: Improvisation and Accompaniment for Social Justice.* Philadelphia: Temple University Press, 2019.

Trans Legislation Tracker. "Tracking the Rise of Anti-trans Bills in the U.S." N.d. *https://translegislation.com/learn.*

US National Park Service. "Carnegie Libraries: The Future Made Bright." Teaching with Historic Places program. N.d. *www.nps.gov/articles/carnegie-libraries-the-future-made-bright-teaching-with-historic-places.htm.*

Villanueva, Edgar. *Decolonizing Wealth: Indigenous Wisdom to Heal Divides and Restore Balance.* Oakland, CA: Berrett-Koehler, 2018.

Wallestad, Anne. "The Four Principles of Purpose-Driven Board Leadership." *Stanford Social Innovation Review.* March 10, 2021. *https://doi.org/10.48558/S4ZJ-Q994.*

Weymouth, Lally. "Foundation Woes the Saga of Henry Ford II: Part Two." *New York Times.* March 12, 1978. *www.nytimes.com/1978/03/12/archives/foundation-woes-the-saga-of-henry-ford-ii-part-two-ford-ford.html.*

White, Lem, and Keiko Murase. "Building Power, Building Wealth: The Value of Community-Driven Models." *Nonprofit Quarterly.* June 22, 2022. *https://nonprofitquarterly.org/building-power-building-wealth-the-value-of-community-driven-models.*

Williams, Patricia J. *The Alchemy of Race and Rights: Diary of a Law Professor.* Cambridge, MA: Harvard University Press, 1991.

World Economic Forum. *Global Risks Report 2023: Insight Report.* Geneva, Switzerland: World Economic Forum, January 11, 2023. *www3.weforum.org/docs/WEF_Global_Risks_Report_2023.pdf.*

INDEX

ACKNOWLEDGMENTS AND GRATITUDES

This book has had a magic to it. From when it was just a kernel of an idea to now, whenever the book has needed something, someone with that thing (wisdom, resources, experience, expertise, moral support, and more) has appeared in my life ready to meet that need.

My first and biggest gratitude is to my family: my mother, Manisha Abichandani, my partner, Anand Adiga, and my daughter, Sumi Adiga. This book exists because of how the three of you supported me and made this possible—I am so grateful for your love and our family.

I asked Maya Trabin to be my editor early in the process of writing this book, and I am so glad she said yes! Maya's role evolved from editor to accomplice to friend. I am forever grateful for her brilliance, skill, humor, curiosity, and her deep commitment to a more just future.

I am grateful to the North Atlantic Books team who brought passion, care, and expertise to this project. My gratitude to Tim McKee, Jasmine Respess, Janelle Ludowise, Julia Sadowski, and Bevin Donahue for their expert guidance and care. Thank you, Rachel Berger, for your excellent work on the visuals in this book.

Writing a book is a resource-intensive process. I share my deep gratitude to the Surdna Foundation, and Don Chen and Sophy Yem, for their generous support. Thank you to the National Center for Family Philanthropy, where I am a fellow, and especially Nick Tedesco, Miki Akimoto, Jason Born, and Daria Teutonico for their heartfelt support. A warm thank you to Cassie Robinson and Sophia Parker at Joseph Rowntree Foundation for inviting me into the Emerging Futures community, and Gwyneth Tripp and Glen Galaich at the Stupski Foundation for your support.

To my Solidaire Network community, a special thank you to Vini Bhansali, Ingrid Benedict, Sam Vinal, Marlena Sonn, Cory Pohley, Lori Holmes, and Mzima Scadeng. Your partnership and support made this book possible, and I am so grateful! To members of the Solidaire Network, thank you for modeling a philanthropy steeped in love, solidarity, and a beautiful bold vision of justice.

This book draws on lessons learned working alongside so many inspiring and cherished colleagues over the past two decades, including from my Third Wave Fund family Vivien Labaton, Kalpana Krishnamurthy, Rye Young, and so many others. At the Proteus Fund I share my gratitude to Meg Gage, Paul Di Donato, for their support of the RISE Together Fund, and to Rana Elmir and Shireen Zaman for their visionary leadership of it. I am grateful to my GSF family for so many years of innovative funding (and fun!) together: Holly Bartling, Desiree Flores, Elaine Mui, Bill Repplinger, and GSF board members, including Eliot Estrin, Gabriella Zhuang-Estrin, Jesse Estrin, Peter Halby, Will Halby, Marcie Musser, Robert Musser, Annabel Snidow, and Robin Snidow. Thank you, Vini Bhansali, Sarita Gupta, Silvia Henriquez, Kierra Johnson, Crystal Plati, Robby Rodriguez, and Dr. Carmen Rojas, for your leadership and partnership. I am grateful to trusted grantee partners across all of these organizations who model courage, vision, and transformation, and who have been my biggest teachers, inspiring my efforts to transform philanthropy, so that their work will be funded abundantly.

This book is a love letter to the many leaders who are forging a new era of philanthropy, modeling how we can redistribute resources and build the more just future we need. This list is inclusive of people who shared their stories and insights with me and who share community: Tegan Acton, Nwamaka Agbo, Gabriela Alcalde, Jamie Allison, Carrie Avery, Rini Banerjee, Elizabeth Barajas-Román, Fred Blackwell, Jen Ching, Chloe Cockburn, Julian Corner, Jara Dean-Coffey, Ellen Dorsey, Farhad Ebrahimi, Bridgit Antoinette Evans, Eileen Farbman, Anna Fink, Aria Florant, Jason Franklin, Crystal Hayling, Taryn Higashi, Rachel Humphrey, Sandy Ho, Pia Infante, Isis Krause, Daniel Lau, Solomé Lemma, Phil Li, Sara

Lomelin, Dwayne Marsh, Nichole June Maher, Retta Morris, Iara Peng, Emma Pompetti, Regan Pritzker, Pamela Ross, Dr. Yanique Redwood, Shaady Salehi, Alex Saingchin, Jocelyn Sargent, Molly Schultz Hafid, Dennis Quirin, Pamela Shifman, Brenda Solórzano, Rusty Stahl, Aaron Tanaka, Aditi Vaidya, Monika Kalra Varma, Lori Villarosa, Gloria Walton, Marcus Walton, Nat Chioke Williams, and Akaya Windwood.

A special thank you to a subset of this inspiring community—friends who read early drafts, shared generous feedback, pushed my thinking, and made this book better: Lisa Cowan, Ginger Daniel, Mandy Van Deven, Jackie Mahendra, Bailey Malone, Joan Minieri, Maria Mottola, Joseph Phelan, Phuong Quach, Ryan Senser, Purvi Shah, and Nick Tedesco.

I am grateful for the community I found with fellow writers, including Vanessa Daniel, Sujatha Jesudason, and Eveline Shen. Thank you to Ariane Conrad for the Storia Summit experience and to my fellow Storia writers. A special thank-you to Minal Hajratwala for creating the Unicorn Authors Club and for your expert coaching. Mia Birdsong, Deepa Iyer, Jungwon Kim, and Rachel Neumann, thank you for sharing advice and support on this journey.

I imagine books as being in conversation, both with their readers and with other books. Two books in particular inspired this one: Tim Snyder's *On Tyranny* has been on my desk since 2017.[1] His book takes hard-won lessons about tyranny and brings them into today's context, in a brief and urgent book that lets us learn from one another. Patricia Williams's *The Alchemy of Race and Rights* inspired me to go to law school and has been with me through every move since 1997.[2] Williams departs from the authoritative and anonymous tone of legal scholarship and writes in the multiplicity of her identities as a poet, critic, scholar, lawyer, and Black woman. Patricia Williams inspired me to write this book in my own voice. Tim Snyder inspired me to keep it brief.

I owe a particular debt to writers who have excavated philanthropy as a symptom of extreme inequality. I am grateful to the INCITE! Women of Color Against Violence, authors of *The Revolution Will Not Be Funded;* Edgar Villanueva, author of *Decolonizing Wealth: Indigenous Wisdom to Heal Divides and Restore Balance;* and Anand Giridharadas, author of *Winners Take All: The Elite Charade of Changing the World* for shining a spotlight onto the flawed origins of philanthropy and the sector's limits today as an engine for effective change-making.[3] I was able to focus this book on where we go from here because of the work these books did to help us understand where we are.

Finally, I am so grateful to dear friends that provided abundant cheering-on as I wrote this book, including Monisha Bajaj, Ginger Daniel, Azi Khalili, Monique Mehta, Purvi Shah, and Susan Shah.

ABOUT THE AUTHOR

Dimple Abichandani is a nationally recognized philanthropic leader, writer, and lawyer. A lifelong student of social change, Dimple has spent the last two decades advancing justice by working to transform the collective purpose and practices of philanthropy. A National Center for Family Philanthropy Fellow, she has been recognized with a Scrivner Award for Creative Grantmaking for her significant contributions to the field of philanthropy. Dimple serves on the board of directors of Solidaire Network, and on the steering committee of the Trust-Based Philanthropy Project. Dimple lives with her family in the San Francisco Bay Area, where she advises donors and funders on how to transform wealth into a more just future. *A New Era of Philanthropy* is her first book.

ABOUT
NORTH ATLANTIC BOOKS

North Atlantic Books (NAB) is an independent, nonprofit publisher committed to a bold exploration of the relationships between mind, body, spirit, and nature. Founded in 1974, NAB aims to nurture a holistic view of the arts, sciences, humanities, and healing. To make a donation or to learn more about our books, authors, events, and newsletter, please visit www.northatlanticbooks.com.